Peadar Cowan (1903–62): Westmeath GAA administrator and political maverick

Maynooth Studies in Local History

SERIES EDITOR Raymond Gillespie

This volume is one of five short books published in the Maynooth Studies in Local History series in 2021. Like their predecessors they range widely over the local experience in the Irish past. Chronologically they range across the 19th century and into the 20th century but they focus on problems that reappeared in almost every period of Irish history. They chronicle the experiences of individuals grappling with their world from the Cork surgeon, Denis Brenan Bullen, in the early 19th century to the politician and GAA administrator Peadar Cowan in the 20th century. From a different perspective they resurrect whole societies under stress from the rural tensions in Knock, Co. Mayo, to the impact of the Famine on Sir William Palmer's estates in Mayo. A rather different sort of institution under stress, Dublin's cattle market, provides the framework for charting the final years of the world that depended on that institution. Geographically they range across the length of the country from Dublin to Cork and westwards into Mayo. Socially they move from those living on the margins of society in Knock through to the prosperous world of the social elite in Cork. In doing so they reveal diverse and complicated societies that created the local past and present the range of possibilities open to anyone interested in studying that past. Those possibilities involve the dissection of the local experience in the complex and contested social worlds of which it is part as people strove to preserve and enhance their positions within their local societies. It also reveals the forces that made for cohesion in local communities and those that drove people apart, whether through large scale rebellion or through acts of inter-personal violence. Such studies of local worlds over such long periods are vital for the future since they not only stretch the historical imagination but provide a longer perspective on the evolution of society in Ireland and help us to understand more fully the complex evolution of the Irish experience. These works do not simply chronicle events relating to an area within administrative or geographically determined boundaries, but open the possibility of understanding how and why particular regions had their own personality in the past. Such an exercise is clearly one of the most exciting challenges for the future and demonstrates the vitality of the study of local history in Ireland.

Like their predecessors, these five short books are reconstructions of the socially diverse worlds of the poor as well as the rich, women as well as men, the geographical marginal of Mayo as well as those located near the centre of power. They reconstruct the way in which those who inhabited those worlds lived their daily lives, often little affected by the large themes that dominate the writing of national history. In addressing these issues, studies such as those presented in these short books, together with their predecessors, are at the forefront of Irish historical research and represent some of the most innovative and exciting work being undertaken in Irish history today. They also provide models that others can follow up and adapt in their own studies of the Irish past. In such ways will we understand better the regional diversity of Ireland and the social and cultural basis for that diversity. They, with their predecessors, convey the vibrancy and excitement of the world of Irish local history today.

Maynooth Studies in Local History: Number 151

Peadar Cowan (1903–62): Westmeath GAA administrator and political maverick

Tom Hunt

FOUR COURTS PRESS

Set in 10pt on 12pt Bembo by
Carrigboy Typesetting Services for
FOUR COURTS PRESS LTD
7 Malpas Street, Dublin 8, Ireland
www.fourcourtspress.ie
and in North America for
FOUR COURTS PRESS
c/o IPG, 814 N Franklin St, Chicago, IL 60610

ISBN 978–1–84682–970–3

Printed in Ireland
by SprintPrint, Dublin.

Contents

Acknowledgments

This work would have been impossible without the support of archivists and librarians. I would like to express my appreciation to the staffs of the following institutions: the Military Archives at Cathal Brugha Barracks in Rathmines, Dublin; the National Library of Ireland, Kildare Street, Dublin; the University College Dublin School of History and Archives at Belfield; the archives of the Gaelic Athletic Association in Croke Park, and the staff of the Local Studies section at the Westmeath County Library, Mullingar. Thanks also to Willie Penrose, Dick Stokes, Eithne MacDermott, Johann Farrelly and Jonathan Smyth for various conversations, suggestions and directions. Thanks also to Professor Raymond Gillespie for inviting me to contribute to these latest volumes of the Maynooth Studies in Local History.

As always thanks to Mary for providing the space and opportunity for historical research and writing.

Introduction

Eamon Dunphy, in his autobiography *The rocky road*, explains in some detail how the Dunphy family were saved from eviction from their one-roomed abode on Richmond Road, Drumcondra. Dunphy explains that a Dublin solicitor, Peadar Cowan, was responsible for the intervention that saved the family. Peg Dunphy, in particular, was a determined lady and chose to challenge the terms of the eviction notice that arrived from some all-powerful and anonymous landlord. She made an appointment to see Peadar Cowan and arrived in the solicitor's Capel Street offices accompanied by her two sons, Eamon and Kevin. The former was an observant child and judged people by how they reacted to his parents. The response varied from 'respect to indifference to annoyance or contempt'. According to Dunphy's account, Cowan 'cut an eccentric figure' dressed in 'an Aran sweater, with sandals and baggy trousers', but he was 'courteous, respectfully gentle'. He quickly read the eviction notice, established that the Dunphy family were up-to-date with their rent and that no alternative accommodation was available. He explained that the justice system was there to protect families from exploitation and immediately volunteered to represent the family free of charge in the Four Courts in what Dunphy considered to be the 'first real crisis of our lives'. 'Say a prayer for me' was Cowan's one demand. Cowan was professionalism personified on the day of the court: 'He was spruced up with a suit and tie and proper pair of shoes'. He outlined the Dunphy case, 'speaking quietly with real conviction': 'Decent people. Hard-working father. Pay their rent. Boys at good local school. Living at this address for more than ten years'. The presiding judge was convinced, the application for eviction refused and Cowan had preserved for the Dunphy family 'a way of life that, though materially modest, was in many other ways immensely rich'.[1]

The young Dunphy was not to know that the man who rescued the family was one of the most controversial politicians of the age and a man of many parts, a Gaelic Athletic Association (GAA) volunteer in an earlier career, a former Irish army officer, a former Labour Party activist, a founder member of Clann na Poblachta, a member of Dáil Éireann, a radical challenger of the consensus and a lawyer. The episode described epitomizes many aspects of Cowan's career: his concern for the underprivileged and marginalized of society; his willingness to provide legal representation without charge; his concern for social justice and his eagerness to challenge vested interests. He was one of the first to draw attention to the plight of travellers for instance. In a letter to the *Irish Press* he drew attention to the plight of itinerants in the Ballyfermot area and called on the government or the Red Cross to provide a winter camp for them 'where comfort, education, advice and help could be given, and perhaps, a new way of life opened up to them. It is our duty to do something practicable for the distressed Irish'.[2]

Described as 'one of the most individualistic and colourful figures in Irish political life for about two decades' in an obituary following his death, Cowan is a relatively unknown figure in Irish history despite some significant contributions made over a forty-year period.[3] His role in Clann na Poblachta is examined in detail by Eithne MacDermott, Kevin Rafter and David McCullagh. Eithne MacDermott in *Clann na Poblachta* variously describes Cowan as emblematic, sardonic, an able administrator, pugnacious and truculent, strong willed, a true iconoclast and a provoker of mischief in the course of her detailed examination of the party history and of Cowan's role in that history.[4] According to Kevin Rafter in *The Clann*, Peadar Cowan (with Noel Hartnett) was 'central to Clann's efforts to put down roots in the various constituencies as well as identifying people to stand as candidates'.[5] David McCullagh's focus in *A makeshift majority* is on Cowan's short role in the inter-party government of 1948–51.[6] J.H. Whyte, in his seminal study *Church & state in modern Ireland, 1923–1979*, provides a detailed analysis of Cowan's singular role in the Dáil debate that followed Noël Browne's resignation as Minister for Health following the mother and child scheme debacle.[7] His role in the Labour Party is less well documented and while Brian Cowen merits a mention in *Making the difference: the Irish Labour Party 1912–2012*, Peadar Cowan is absent, despite his contribution to the party in the late 1930s.[8]

Newspapers, both local and national, provide the main primary sources for this examination of Peadar Cowan's career. The local press, especially the *Westmeath Examiner*, the *Meath Chronicle* and the *Drogheda Independent*, were particularly valuable for tracing Cowan's GAA involvement, and his political activity at constituency level. The national newspapers were important for exploring national issues and political debate. Cowan's deliberations frequently appeared on the letters page of various newspapers as he defended his sometimes controversial viewpoints or rejected allegations regarding his political beliefs, particularly the charges levelled by Fianna Fáil's character-assassin-in-chief, Seán MacEntee, that Cowan was a communist. In the absence of radio access and long before the onset of television, letters to the newspapers were the principal means by which political arguments were publicly aired. And as Eithne MacDermott has observed 'they enjoyed the sort of prominence reserved today for the more popular radio or television interviews or debates'.[9] The Dáil Éireann debates were the principal source for the parliamentary career of Cowan while the papers of Seán MacEntee include a file entitled 'Revolutionary and subversive organisations' in which Peadar Cowan features prominently. The minute books of the Westmeath county GAA committee provide useful material on his work for the GAA in the county.

The first chapter of this study deals briefly with Peadar Cowan's involvement in the war of independence and his career as an army officer. The main focus of this chapter is on his extraordinary contribution to the development of the Gaelic Athletic Association (GAA) in Westmeath, which is part of the hidden history of Cowan's career. It is unacknowledged in any assessment of his career including his biographical entry in the *Dictionary of Irish biography*. The second chapter deals briefly with his association with radical politics in the early 1930s, including his links with Saor Éire and the Republican Congress. The primary focus of this chapter is on his work with the Labour Party. He unsuccessfully represented the party on four occasions in general elections in the Meath–Westmeath constituency and became Director of Organization for the party in 1942. These were troubled times for the party and Cowan eventually resigned from the party and established the short-lived socialist movement The Vanguard before rejoining the party in 1945. His short career with Clann na Poblachta is examined in the third chapter. A founder member of the party and its financial director, he brought valuable administrative and political experience to the fledgling party. He was one of the 10 members of the party elected to Dáil Éireann in 1948 but his tenure as a party member was short lived and he was expelled from the party within four months of entering Dáil Éireann. Peadar Cowan was elected to Dáil Éireann for the Dublin North-East constituency on 4 February 1948, was re-elected as an independent deputy in 1951 but lost his seat in the election to the 15th Dáil held on 18 May 1954. As a member of the Dáil he was a regular, able and courageous contributor to debates and his most notable contributions are examined in chapter four. This study concludes with an examination of the final difficult personal and professional years of Cowan's life and concludes with an overall assessment of his career.

1. Army officer and GAA administrator

COWAN THE ARMY OFFICER

Peadar Cowan was born on 23 October 1903, in Lacken, Ballinagh, Co. Cavan, the eldest son of farm-labourer Thomas Cowan, and his wife Annie. As a teenager, he took part in the War of Independence as a member of the Ballinagh Company of the Cavan Brigade of the Irish Republican Army (IRA) prior to his arrest and imprisonment. His membership of the IRA has been certified from 1 April 1920.[1] He was incarcerated in Crumlin Road jail in Belfast for thirteen months where, according to An t-Óglác, the enthusiast for football and handball 'kept himself in practice by kicking his cell door.' He supported the Anglo-Irish Treaty of 1921 and joined the 1st Midland Division of the new national army on 10 February 1922 from a home address of Cashel, Ballinagh, Co. Cavan. He was initially based in the Seán Connolly Barracks, Longford, where he held the rank of second-lieutenant. He was later promoted to the rank of captain, which was subsequently reduced to the rank of second-lieutenant when the army was reduced in size after the Civil War. He was posted to Custume Barracks in Athlone where he was responsible for the reorganization of the military in the town. He was again promoted to the rank of captain shortly before he resigned from the army in September 1931.[2]

Cowan later provided an insight into the process by which the decision to support or reject the terms of the Anglo-Irish Treaty was reached in an address delivered to the Fabian Society in Trinity College Dublin. He was in Crumlin Road jail when he learned that a treaty had been signed, a time when he was not 'very experienced in the world'. At the age of 18, Cowan and his comrades of a similar age were required to make a decision on the future of the country with no precedent or experience of the world of politics to inform them. According to this account, personality rather than principle influenced Cowan's decision. He recalled a series of meetings at battalion, brigade and divisional level at which each volunteer formulated his own response to the agreement. The personality of the commanding officer was crucial, Cowan explained, in reaching a decision: 'If he was a man of personality; if he had a distinguished record; if he had taken a prominent part in the fight, naturally the majority of the company would support him. The vote was taken. In that moment the decision was made for one side or the other'. Cowan was of the opinion that 'there was no power in the country that could have stopped the Civil War we had in 1922' as the volunteers were not under the control of the civil authorities.

The lesson to be drawn from this was clear: 'The army in any country should be under the strict and rigid control of the civil authority … The army is a dangerous thing unless it is controlled. If I take pride in anything it is that I did help in my little way to build up in this country, a force that is loyal and under the strict control of the government of the country'.[3] Disillusionment with government management of the army influenced his decision to opt for an alternative career path. In 1938, he spoke of how the army was repeatedly reorganized and reduced in the period between 1924 and 1932 so that only 'a remnant that was neither an army nor a police force remained'. The final period of the Cosgrave administration 'was disastrous for the army' and the 'general feeling in military circles was that the government had decided on the abolition of the army'.[4]

Peadar Cowan was introduced to the world of sports' administration through his association with the Army Athletic Association (AAA) where he represented the Western Command at its executive meetings and annual conventions.[5] The central role played by sport in the army was given institutional recognition on 31 March 1923 with the formation of the AAA. According to *An t-Óglác*, the official newspaper of the Irish Free State Army, athletics assisted 'materially in bringing about that condition of physical fitness essential to the complete efficiency of the soldier and stimulate a healthy sporting spirit amongst the men'. The army scheme for sport was 'carefully constructed and comprehensively designed' so that the soldiers could 'secure plenty of variety in their athletic training without having recourse to other than Gaelic games'. In the belief that the army should provide the backbone of the Irish-Ireland movement, the four sports designated as foreign by the GAA – soccer, rugby, cricket and hockey – were excluded from the army curriculum. An editorial in *An t-Óglác* explained that

> The young Irishmen in the Army are the bone and sinew of the country and will play a vitally important part in the creation of the Gaelic State to which we all look forward. They will be all the better citizens of that State in consequence of the training they receive in the Army, and the fostering of a love of clean, healthy sport will be by no means the least valuable part of their military education.

The case for the exclusion of the four sports was made by Eoin O'Duffy who explained that 'The [GAA] games were Irish of the Irish, and it would be a sad day when the Irish Army left aside their own games for games of foreign origin'. The exclusion decision was unanimous: the Chief of Staff, Peadar MacMahon, thanked the representatives of the GAA and explained that 'The Army should be the backbone of the Irish-Ireland movement, and should contribute of its stock to make Ireland a truly Gaelic State'.[6] The AAA retained the exclusion rule until 1943 when the Minister for Defence, Oscar Traynor, reconstituted the AAA with an executive committee composed of senior army officers. As a result the AAA became an official army body with its decisions now the responsibility of the Minister for Defence. One of the first decisions made by this new executive was to officially recognize and cater for the playing of soccer and rugby in the army. Peadar Cowan was one of the first to draw public attention to what he referred to as 'a significant and sinister change of government attitude towards Gaelic games' and at the annual GAA congress of 1943 led the opposition to this decision as the GAA passed a motion calling on the army to reverse the decision.[7]

PEADAR COWAN: THE GAA ADMINISTRATOR

Peadar Cowan emerged from this military milieu to become one of the most important and able administrators in the history of the Westmeath GAA. The philosophy influenced some of his decision making as Westmeath chairman. At the 1929 county convention, for example, he refused to allow any discussion on a motion from the Mullingar Club that sought to remove the GAA ban on attending 'foreign games' and ruled that regardless of the convention's decision, the ban would be retained by the association.

Lt Peadar Cowan was a founder member and secretary of the Athlone Emmet's club, a club organized by army officers based in the town but with membership open to all.[8] He first attended a Westmeath county committee meeting as a delegate of the Athlone club on 30 July 1926. Seven months later, on 30 January 1927, at just 24 years of age, he was elected chairman of the board and he began a remarkable decade of service to the county that ended on 20 December 1936 when he retired from the position of honorary secretary. Peadar Cowan also represented Westmeath at Leinster Council level and at the GAA's annual congress. The circumstances surrounding his election are indicative of the advanced stage of disorganization that existed in the Westmeath GAA world of the time. At the convention, the incumbent chairman Lar Leech was not present, the secretary's report was not available for the delegates and no agenda had been circularised. Despite these irregularities, the delegates decided to continue with the meeting and Cowan was elected chairman, defeating J.J. Carey (Rochfortbridge) for the post (64–28). In his ten years association with Westmeath GAA, he transformed the organization within the county. When he was first elected the county competed at junior level in both hurling and football. All-Ireland junior titles in football (1929) and hurling (1936) secured Westmeath's promotion to senior status in both codes in Leinster and were marked almost immediately by qualification for Leinster senior finals. The 1929 All-Ireland junior football title was won on 22 February 1930 in Croke Park when London were defeated. This was the first time in history that the county won an All-Ireland title and a special period of training was organised prior to the final.[9] The county transitioned to senior ranks without much difficulty. In

(6)

Cumann na ₅Cleás Lút n₅aeóealaċ Connuae
na h-Iar Mióe.

BYE-LAWS FOR THE BETTER GOVERNMENT AND CONTROL OF THE GAELIC ATHLETIC ASSOCIATION IN COUNTY WESTMEATH.

PASSED AT CONVENTION—JANUARY, 1929.

1—The County Committee shall consist of the Chairman, Vice-Chairman, Secretary, Treasurer, Registrar, Representatives on the Leinster Council, and one Representative of each Affiliated Club in the County.

2—The County Committee shall be responsible for the selection of teams to represent the County in inter-county and inter-provincial matches, but they may delegate this responsibility to a sub-committee, appointed by them.

3—The affiliation fee of 12s. shall be paid to the Treasurer of the County Committee by each Club on or before 14th February in the current year.

4—A current account in the name of the County Committee shall be kept in the Mullingar Branch of the National Bank. This account shall be operated by the Vice-Chairman and Treasurer.

5—A honorarium of £25 plus 10% of the profits on the year's working shall be given to the Secretary annually from the funds of the County Committee.

6—A sum not exceeding £5 at a time may be allotted for incidental expenses to the Secretary, who will obtain and retain receipts in respect of any portion thereof expended by him. Any balance on hands will be lodged in the Bank during the last week of December.

7—Save as otherwise provided for in these Bye-Laws no expenditure shall be incurred or accounts paid without the sanction of a meeting of the County Committee.

8—A statement of the Financial position of the County Committee shall be read at each meeting immediately after the Minutes of the previous meeting have been signed.

9—Ordinary Meetings of the County Committee shall be held at 8 p.m. on the second Friday of each month during the period May to October, inclusive, and as often as may be necessary during the remainder of the year. At such meetings eight shall form a quorum. A person attending on behalf of the member must be in possession of a proxy from that member.

1. Bye-laws for the better management of the GAA in Westmeath, 1929

Cowan's words, 1931 'was one continuous series of triumphs' for the county's senior footballers highlighted by the defeat of Kilkenny and Dublin to reach the Leinster senior final for the first time. Although beaten by Kildare 'our team made a splendid impression on the Gaels of Leinster by their brilliant, clean, spectacular and characteristically Gaelic display. They were a credit not only to themselves and to this county but to Ireland'.[10]

'Hurling which was essentially the national game was in a rather backward position in Westmeath', he told delegates at the 1930 annual convention but 'he intended to take an intense interest in the game' and it was planned to raise the standard of hurling to the same high pitch as football had reached.[11] The 1936 season showcased the progress of the sport as the Westmeath team chalked up ten straight wins, four in the Leinster league and six in the Leinster and All-Ireland junior championship that ended with the defeat of Waterford (2-5 to 3-1) in the final played in Croke Park on 13 September 1936. After the match, Westmeath adjourned to Barry's Hotel where the congratulations poured in. The team returned by train to Mullingar later in the evening. A fireworks display lit up the sky and fog signals boomed out as the train approached the station.[12] Westmeath followed this in 1937 by qualifying for a Leinster senior hurling final for the first and only time.

A start was made at improving the county's administration at the convention of 1928 when the first eight motions on the agenda were proposed by the Athlone GAA Club, the club of Peadar Cowan, and were designed to create a more efficient system. These included provision for the defraying of the expenses incurred by the chairman and secretary and one that read 'that any club and the registered members thereof owing any money to the county board be considered suspended until such time as their liability is cleared'.[13] The improvement in administration was further signalled in 1929 with the publication of a booklet of 'Bye-laws for the better government and control of the Gaelic Athletic Association in County Westmeath' (fig.1). This publication was also designed to reduce the number of 'frivolous objections' which Cowan believed were a product of 'the carelessness and ignorance of club secretaries with their knowledge of rules and bye-laws'. He promised a circular to educate club officers on such matters. The published booklet contained forty-three bye-laws setting down the essentials for the good order and management of the GAA in the county.[14] The county was also divided into six regions to facilitate games playing and Cowan travelled to each division and explained to the local officials their duties and responsibilities. Cowan presided at a time when objections bedevilled the association and undermined championship progress. He worked hard to eliminate this distraction and at the 1932 convention he explained that the great majority of 'real Gaels' looked for guidelines 'to the spirit rather than to the letter of the rules'. 'Ours is an amateur organization and ... a complicated organization' he explained, 'and in it there is undoubtedly scope for the activities of ill-meaning and selfish individuals who though in the GAA are not of it. But so long as decent, straight, and honest Gaels are in control of the clubs and committees there shall be neither cause for petty objections nor place for petty objectors'. Castlepollard Hurling Club experienced both sides of Cowan's logic; in 1933, the letter of the law was implemented, in 1928 the spirit of the rules was activated when the club failed to field in the hurling county final. This championship was played on a double-round league system and the men from Castlepollard finished four points ahead of the Mullingar Hurling Club in second place. In keeping with the decision taken at the county board meeting of 28 February 1928, a final was scheduled between the two clubs and when Castlepollard did not take the field, Cowan later ruled that 'on league rules, Castlepollard were entitled to the medals'.[15] In October 1933, Clonkill were surprisingly and comprehensively defeated by Castlepollard (4-4 to 0-2) in the county senior hurling final.[16] Cowan later declared this match void as the referee had reported both teams were late arriving on the pitch.[17] The hard-line attitude displayed only makes sense when the context of the match is considered. The hurling final was the opening-act to the final of the Cusack Park tournament between Dublin and Kildare, the two victorious teams on the opening day of Cusack Park, and thus it gave Westmeath GAA national exposure. The supposed tardiness of the hurling clubs in taking the field reflected poorly on this image. There was a wildness associated with the GAA at this time and maintaining discipline in games was not an easy task. Impartiality and an ability to maintain law and order were essential requirements for a referee during this era. Peadar Cowan earned a reputation as an excellent referee and made himself available on a regular basis to referee matches, especially those that had the potential to be tempestuous. He officiated at a number of county finals in both hurling and football including the Westmeath senior football finals of 1928 and 1934 and the senior hurling final of 1935. He was also recruited to officiate at key matches outside the county and was in charge of the whistle at the Offaly senior football final and replay between Rhode and Tullamore in 1928. He also refereed at inter-county level.[18]

Despite the financial requirements enshrined in the bye-laws, Cowan, on his election as secretary in 1932, inherited liabilities of almost £260 and warned clubs that much closer control of the county finances was required 'and much more rigid economies would have to be effected' if the finances of the board were to be placed on a satisfactory footing. As a result, the deficit was wiped out in the course of the 1932 season when income exceeded expenditure by £293.[19] The expenditure for 1932 included an *ex-gratia* payment of £3 to county hurler Patrick Lenihan of the Delvin club. Lenihan had claimed for the loss of an overcoat valued at £3, shoes to the value of £1 5s. and gloves worth 15s. These items of clothing were stolen from the hotel and dressing room at Tullamore as Westmeath contested the Leinster junior hurling semi-final.[20] The financial performance during Cowan's period in office during the 1930s is illustrated in Table 1.

Table 1. Income and expenditure of Westmeath GAA, 1930–6

Year	Income (£ s. d.)	Expenditure (£ s. d.)	Profit/Loss (£ s. d.)
1930	1053	1095	− 42
1931	610.17.11	691.13.7	− 80.15.8
1932	831.16.4	538.15.5	+ 293.0.11
1933	1628.16.4	919.15.9	+ 709.0.7
1934	665.11.6	584.12.9	+ 80.18.9
1935	881.5.0	900.15.0	− 19.10.0
1936	1052.7.7	812.11.10	+ 239.15.9

Source: County board minute book.

A competitive programme of games of staggering proportions was introduced during Peadar Cowan's terms in office, a progression partly designed as a revenue-generating exercise for both clubs and county. The basic programme was restructured in 1929 when a league competition was introduced, for senior and junior clubs in both codes, in which clubs played against each other on a home and away basis. In 1931, a primary schools committee was established and competitions, in hurling and football, began in the primary schools. In 1934, nine senior football teams, six senior hurling teams, thirty-three junior football and sixteen junior hurling teams took part in the championship, an increase of twelve on 1933. Record gate receipts of £352 were collected.[21] This work attracted national attention and 'Green Flag', the GAA correspondent of the *Irish Press*, suggested that if other counties made comparable progress to Westmeath's 1934 advance 'this will certainly be a record period in the life of the GAA'.[22]

Remarkably, Cowan's achievements were accomplished while he conducted vendettas against many of his fellow board officers and the truculence which was later to be a characteristic feature of his political career was given a public staging for the first time. He had a particular difficulty with the county secretary, Peter Kelleghan. Cowan survived two attempts by the Mullingar GAA Club to oust him from office on the basis that he was no longer a member of a club and that he resided outside the county. After his election as chairman at the annual convention on 27 January 1929, the issue of his legality to hold the position was raised by Kelleghan who claimed he was reflecting the concern of the clubs of the county. However, in the subsequent discussion, Kelleghan was left isolated and unsupported by club delegates. Cowan claimed he was prepared to resign if there was an issue over his legality and only allowed his name to go forward because of the fresh scheme introduced to run the championship. The position was inconvenient for him but 'he intended to put the scheme in motion and endeavour to put the County Board on a solid financial footing'.[23]

Cowan was transferred to Dublin in March 1928, a transfer that was 'deeply regretted in the town [Athlone], particularly in Gaelic circles' the *Westmeath Independent* reported.[24] At the annual convention held on 19 January 1930, he informed delegates that 'the secretarial end of the business was not satisfactory for one reason or another, which I cannot explain ... The secretary has developed animosity towards me and the result was that he did not keep me in sufficient touch with the affairs of the board'. He then went on to identify Patrick Carey 'as one man who offered very loyal support'. This was a blatant piece of electioneering on behalf of Carey who was nominated to challenge Kelleghan for the position of county secretary. Kelleghan, of course, rejected Cowan's claims and responded in a similar vein. Cowan's attempt to have him removed as county secretary failed as Kelleghan comfortably defeated Carey in the election for the post.[25] The Mullingar club's efforts to have Cowan removed did not end in Westmeath, the legality of his election was appealed to the Leinster Council, requesting that in the 'interests of the games in Westmeath, Lt Cowan's election should be declared null and void'. Patrick Carey defended Cowan's election and explained that Cowan 'went forward for election because he was forced to do so by the most prominent and the most active Gaels in the County'. The appeal was dismissed, the Leinster chairman ruled that as Cowan was an out-going officer, he was a member of the county committee and consequently eligible for election. The GAA's Central Council also rejected an appeal of the Leinster decision at its meeting on 29 March 1930.[26] As a Westmeath delegate, Cowan played a prominent role at the association's annual congress in 1930 and was responsible for the introduction of a rule change that was described as 'revolutionary'. It empowered the county committees to warn or fine clubs for breaches of rules and was in part designed to put an end to the number of 'trivial, irritating and ridiculous objections', an issue that Cowan felt very strongly about. In effect, the rule change meant that teams that won on the field were no longer in danger of losing the match except 'for roughness, unpunctuality or illegal constitution'.[27] The congress was something of a personal triumph for Cowan. Two Roscommon motions seeking the transfer of the Athlone Urban District or the portion of Athlone west of the river Shannon to Roscommon for GAA purposes were overwhelmingly defeated. This battle was subsequently lost at the 1934 GAA congress when the portion of the town west of the Shannon was transferred, a decision reaffirmed at the 1935 congress.[28] A motion he proposed to award Westmeath £50 in additional expenses to cater for the extra expenses incurred in preparation for the All-Ireland final was successful and a Westmeath motion that proposed a rule change preventing non-residents or non-natives of a county from seeking office or re-election to a post 'had the invidious distinction of not being reached and so fell through'.[29] The feuding with the county secretary continued at the 1932 convention where a loss of £80 on the year's activities was reported. He warned delegates that 'we cannot afford to continue expending money on the scale we have been spending it in the last two years. There has to be a new, a better and more effective control of our finances'. As Kelleghan also held the position of treasurer there was a clear implication that he was incompetent. Cowan announced his resignation from the chairman's post but he was 'not anxious to sever connections with the county committee'. Difficult decisions that were essential to recoup the heavy losses were required to place the county on a sound financial basis. 'If you think I can be of any assistance to you in that work', he told the delegates, 'do not hesitate to say so. I am at your disposal'. The delegates accepted Cowan's offer, and by a margin of 72 votes to 49, he was elected honorary secretary defeating his nemesis Peter Kelleghan, who however was unanimously elected treasurer. In his acceptance address, Cowan called on the clubs 'not to allow political differences to disrupt their harmony' and advised that he was not going to claim 'a single penny' of the honorarium available.[30]

Although a pragmatist in his interpretation of the GAA's Official Guide on occasions, Cowan was a traditionalist in his understanding of the role and values of the GAA. These views were expressed in his address at the 1932 convention when he pointed out the need to

> Continually guard against the idea, unfortunately too prevalent, that the GAA is only an athletic organisation. The GAA has a spiritual or cultural mission and the cultivation of our National Games is a powerful means towards its real object, the making of Ireland not free merely, but Gaelic as well. If this object was kept clearly in mind there would be an end to much of the confused thinking and nonsensical talking about the GAA with which we are all too familiar.[31]

However, the Gaelicization of Ireland would not be brought about simply by the playing of Irish games, Cowan explained, as he outlined his vision of the ideal Ireland in terms similar to those Eamon de Valera was later to articulate:

> Our ideal is an Irish-speaking Ireland living as far as possible on its own resources, its inhabitants dressed in Irish materials and amused and recreated by Irish games, pastimes, music and customs – an almost self-contained Ireland with its own culture, its own distinctive civilisation. That is the ideal for which we all must strive. It is the end to which all our efforts and activities must be directed ... Our task is a noble one; let us not fail in it.[32]

The address also included a warning against the growth of materialism, 'the yardstick by which all our values are assessed', in what might well have been the first public indication that he was becoming familiar with papal encyclicals and of the anti-capitalist agenda that he was later to champion.

The spirit of the market place is pervading and ever dominating our ideals. This is definitely and decidedly wrong. A Nation and especially a small Nation, shall only endure if its moral basis is sound and if its citizens are permeated by a spirit of righteousness both in private and public life. This ethical standard will be brought about not by precept but by the good example of earnest citizens and I appeal to you Gaels by your example to set for your fellow citizens the highest standard of sensible and unselfish conduct.[33]

DEVELOPING A GAA PARK IN MULLINGAR

In 1930, the Westmeath GAA community embarked on the most ambitious project in the county's history, the development of a GAA park in Mullingar, a development that would encourage 'the promotion of a proper Gaelic spirit amongst the people'. The movement was given considerable impetus in 1930 when a dispute developed between the officers of the GAA and members of the board of the Mullingar Mental Hospital on the right of the GAA to use the mental hospital grounds. Mullingar Soccer Club sought and was granted permission to use the grounds and as a result a dispute developed that culminated in the Westmeath GAA refusing to use the hospital grounds and Mullingar was left without a GAA venue. The committee suffered the considerable embarrassment of being unable to host a Westmeath competition as part of a nationally organized Easter Sunday fund-raising tournament in aid of St Enda's in 1931 because the town's soccer club had obtained the use of the venue for the same day.[34] A suitable, centrally-located area was obtained in February 1932.[35] Shrewdly the county executive organized a public meeting of Mullingar residents shortly after the purchase of the land and this moved the development outside the narrow confines of the Mullingar GAA community to involve the greater body politic of church, state and business community representatives who joined members of the county committee. This committee initiated, supervised and controlled all the work done in connection with the pitch.[36]

The work of draining, levelling, fencing and re-sodding was begun in July 1932 and was soon interrupted by serious labour disputes, which escalated into a full scale riot situation at which the police found it necessary to fire shots into the air to restore order. The contractor hired twelve local men and agreed a weekly rate of pay that was equivalent to the wage of a county council road worker. Work commenced on 11 July 1932 and one week later the labourers sought a wage increase. This demand was refused and strike was threatened and most of the local workers were dismissed and replaced with labourers hired from Longford and the rural districts surrounding Mullingar. Inevitably trouble developed and on Monday 25 July union officials and supporters entered the field and called on the workers to leave. Some fighting took place as workers were attacked and beaten and the police were called to restore order. Work continued the following day with police protection in an extremely tense situation.[37] On Wednesday 27 July people assembled and gradually surrounded the pitch and on a whistle signal, over 300 people described as 'union workers and their supporters' launched an attack on the '28 or 29 workmen engaged by Mr Kilbride'. A riot quickly developed and 'spades, shovels and other things were brought into requisition'. Police arrived and baton charged the attackers who retaliated and a full-scale riot developed that involved police, workers, and their attackers. According to the *Midland Herald* reporter, 'to make matters worse stone-throwing commenced in which, it is stated, women as well as men took part'.[38] The battle raged for almost a half-hour and eventually the police were forced to fire shots into the air to restore order. In September 1932, fifty-nine defendants were brought before the District Court on violence and intimidation charges. The Probation Act was applied in all cases.[39] Work recommenced in October and the dispute, apart from causing considerable delay to the development, also added significantly to the overall cost.[40]

The new park was officially opened on Sunday 16 July 1933; at this stage a sum of £3,284 11s. 8d. had been invested in the project.[41] Public subscriptions were sourced to finance the development. The challenge to raise the necessary finance was approached in a number of different ways. The county was divided into twenty-two districts where the local GAA club was responsible for sourcing subscriptions. The districts contributed £187 or 17 per cent of the total of £1,073 that was subscribed by opening day.[42] Additional donations and grants to the value of £711 was also received. In particular, a £500 grant was received from the Leinster Council and £150 from the Westmeath GAA committee.[43] Later in the year, the Leinster Council awarded an additional grant of £100 and the Westmeath executive provided an extra £450 from the profits of the opening day events. At the end of the year a deficit of £1,643 remained outstanding on the park.[44]

The ceremonies associated with the park opening provided a mixture of the spectacular and the solemn with the football matches designed to showcase the talents of the greatest football teams of the era. The great Kerry 1929–32 four-in-a-row All-Ireland champion team was the marquee attraction.[45] Mindful of the logistics involved in managing the influx of up to 15,000 spectators to the town a number of committees were established to ensure the smooth running of these operations.[46] In an era when the political parade was commonplace, the Sunday events began with a procession that showcased the strength of the Westmeath GAA. A parade of over 2,000 individuals representing schools, clubs and camogie teams moved from the Fair Green through the principal streets of Mullingar and formed a colourful spectacle as it entered the park led by the Confraternity Band as it played the triumphalist anthem 'Faith of our Fathers'. The opening ceremony concluded with the hoisting of the national flag, a salute of bugles and the playing of the National Anthem by the No. 1 Army Band.

The opening events at Mullingar were a public proclamation of the extent to which the interests of the GAA and the Catholic Church had coalesced and provide an example in the context of sport of how, as Vincent Comerford has suggested, 'through wider cultural life and practice, that the Irish Free State and its predominant majority completed the invention of the Irish nation as Catholic'.[47] The presence of the bishop of Meath, Dr Mulvany, and several other ecclesiastical dignitaries affirmed the work of the Westmeath GAA and was an indication of the extent to which the organization had achieved respectability. Dr Mulvany formally opened and blessed the grounds. He was provided with a guard of honour formed by the Catholic boy scouts and pupils of the Mullingar Christian Brothers College, as he made his way to the centre of the field. Dr Mulvany threw in the ball to start the second game, which was refereed by the honorary president of the Westmeath county committee, Fr P. Dunne C.C. In the ceremonies, the presence of representatives of Church and state affirmed the inclusion of the GAA as part of the nation's establishment. Pádraig Ó Caoimh secretary general of the GAA, provided the keynote address on behalf of the GAA; Revd E. Crinion, Peadar Cowan and state solicitor J.E. Wallace, who spoke on behalf of the field committee, also addressed the attendance. These events were followed by a half-hour musical recital delivered by the No. 1 Army Band.[48] The theatre of the day was brought to a spectacular climax with the success of Cowan's novel and imaginative idea of dropping a ball from an aeroplane to start the opening match between Cavan and Kildare. At a time when the daily press carried regular accounts of the deeds of airmen across the world, it is doubtful if a more spectacular exercise could have been devised. The aeroplane, hired at a cost of £3 10s. from Iona Airways, arrived from Dublin, 'something not unlike a bird with huge wings' according to the *Midland Reporter*, manoeuvred over the pitch and succeeded in dropping the match ball between some waiting players.[49] The attraction of the day's entertainment is reflected in the gate receipts of £705 10s. 9d. Based on the admission charge of 1s. over 14,100 paying customers attended the opening day's events in Cusack Park.[50] Celebrations concluded with a ceilí, organized by the Mullingar branch of the Gaelic League. Music was supplied by the Columcille Ceilidhe Band from Dublin 'as heard on wireless in Hospitals Trust sponsored programmes'. Peadar Cowan had an answer for those who criticized the failure to employ Mullingar or Westmeath musicians for the occasion. In typical abrasive manner, he reminded the discontented that the Cusack Park development had cost almost £3,000 'and that the total sum collected in Westmeath for the Park funds, up to the present, does not exceed £400'.[51]

Peadar Cowan's work was complete and at the August county committee meeting he announced his resignation ('happy in the knowledge that our national games and pastimes will continue to progress and prosper in Westmeath') having accomplished his ambitions of putting the county finances in order, eliminating friction and having presided over the Cusack Park development.[52] The members refused to accept his retirement and at the next meeting he agreed to continue until the end of the year, a delay that eventually extended until 1936 as Cowan held the position of honorary secretary in his final three years of involvement in Westmeath GAA affairs.[53] At the August meeting, Peadar Cowan, in a grand gesture that was in many ways typical of the man, issued a general amnesty to all members serving a term of suspension, as a gesture of thanks for the support received in the park development and to mark what he believed was 'a new life for the Association in the county'.[54] In the world of the GAA such gestures normally excluded those serving a suspension based on a breach of the foreign games rule. On this occasion, Cowan was magnanimous.

Peadar Cowan was admitted to practice as a solicitor in October 1936 after four years of study.[55] He retired from his position as Westmeath GAA county secretary at the annual convention on 20 December 1936. His achievements as a GAA administrator in the county were monumental. He became an officer of the board at a time when the county's administration had virtually collapsed. On his leaving, the county had won All-Ireland junior titles in both hurling and football, the administration and finances of the county were placed on a sound footing and Cusack Park in Mullingar was one of the finest GAA venues in provincial Ireland. The quality of the venue combined with Mullingar's central location and Peadar Cowan's influence at national level of the GAA made the town the ideal location for the staging of matches of national importance. Three All-Ireland football semi-finals were hosted in Mullingar during the 1930s as well as a Railway Cup semi-final. Peadar Cowan bequeathed a substantial legacy to the GAA community of the county.[56]

2. Peadar Cowan and the Labour Party

Peadar Cowan's serious immersion in the world of the GAA ended when he retired from his Westmeath position and although he was one of three nominees for the position of president of the GAA in 1943, he did not contest the election. After retiring from the army, he dabbled in fringe politics and was associated with the radical republican group Saor Éire (1931) and with the Republican Congress (1934). The former sought to 'achieve an independent revolutionary leadership for the working class and working farmers towards the overturn in Ireland of British imperialism and its ally, Irish capitalism' and 'to organize and consolidate the republic of Ireland on the basis of the possession and administration by the workers and working farmers of the land, instruments of production, distribution and exchange'. The desire to 'revive and foster the Irish language, culture and games' were also included in the manifesto. The reaction to Saor Éire was predictable and on Sunday, 18 October 1931, it was the subject of episcopal condemnation: it was 'sinful and irreligious ... and frankly Communistic in its aims' and planned to 'impose upon the Catholic soil of Ireland the same materialistic regime with its fanatical hatred of God as now dominates Russia and threatens to dominate Spain'.[1] Saor Éire disappeared within a year but many of its active members re-emerged later in Clann na Poblachta and this engagement represented for some their first steps in a long and tedious path towards political and parliamentary engagement. In addition, several of Saor Éire's social policies reappeared not just as Clann na Poblachta policies but as government policies during the inter-party government's term of office and by the early 1950s many of these ideas were regarded as perfectly legitimate goals in mainstream political thought almost everywhere in Western Europe.[2]

At the IRA Army Convention of 1934 a failed attempt to gain approval for a mass congress of republicans dedicated to the working-class struggle ended with some members setting up such a congress independently. In April, the decidedly anti-Fascist Republican Congress was launched with the declaration 'that a republic of a united Ireland will never be achieved except through a struggle which uproots capitalism on the way'. The Republican Congress made steady progress during the summer of 1934 and attracted a degree of support from an eclectic mix of socialist republicans, communists, labour activists and ordinary workers greater than any previous socialist project. In Dublin and other urban centres members were involved in highlighting the appalling quality of working-class housing and exposing rack-renting landlords. However, the movement suffered a fatal split at its first congress held at Rathmines in September 1934. The delegates were divided on what type of movement the Republican Congress should become and what political objective it should aim to achieve. A majority were committed to the goal of establishing a workers' republic; a significant minority argued that the objective should simply be a republic. On the organizational question the majority view favoured the establishment of a political party; a minority led by Peadar O'Donnell wished to maintain the congress as a united front. Failure to secure the support of the Labour Party, a few weeks later at its annual conference, dealt another blow to the congress.[3]

PEADAR COWAN AND THE LABOUR PARTY

Peadar Cowan eventually found a political home in the Labour Party in the mid-1930s and unsuccessfully contested the general elections of 1937, 1938, 1941 and 1944 for the Meath–Westmeath constituency. He joined, he later explained, because 'he could not stand aside and see the hunger, squalor and misery in this country, while the two big parties were cutting one another's throats'.[4] Peadar Cowan's profile from his Westmeath GAA career made him an attractive candidate to contest the 1937 general election on behalf of the Labour Party in the Meath–Westmeath constituency. He was chosen to contest the election at the Labour Party's constituency conference held at Athboy, Co. Meath, on 16 May 1937. His running mate was John Hayden, a Mullingar member of the Westmeath County Council. Cowan was beginning to rise through the ranks of the party and at this time he was secretary of the Dublin branch of the Dublin Labour Youth Movement, a movement that provided a variety of extra-curricular activities to make the political engagement more attractive. Social and recreational events were organized to supplement the programme of political lectures and debates.[5]

Cowan joined the Labour Party when its policies were at their most radical. In February 1936, the party adopted a constitution that called for a system of government based 'upon the public ownership by the people of all essential sources of wealth' and the organization of 'essential industries ... on the basis of public ownership and democratic control' ... in short 'the establishment in Ireland of a Workers' Republic'.[6] He began his election campaign on 31 May 1937 at a public meeting at Athboy. He promised to campaign on policies and politics 'and would not talk about what individuals had done or what their ancestors had done'. A plebiscite on the adoption of a new constitution for the Irish Free State, Bunreacht na hÉireann, was held in association with the election but Cowan promised that he would not be talking about the constitution or the governor-general or 'any of those high-falutin matters'. A large part of his address was devoted to explaining how the conditions of the working classes had improved as a result of Labour Party pressure on Fianna Fáil. The Housing Act of 1932, for instance, 'admitted to be the finest in Europe', was framed by the Labour Party, he claimed. The party was also influential in the passage of other acts that improved the lot of the marginalized including the unemployed, and widows and orphans. He promised that the Labour Party would work 'for some reorganization' that would give guaranteed prices and guaranteed markets to farmers, a topic he was to return to on a regular basis throughout his career.[7] Since the 1933 general election, a type of confidence and supply arrangement was in place by which the party agreed to 'give full support to measures which are in accordance with the national and economic policy as laid down in its programme'.[8] At his election rally in Mullingar, on 20 June, the labour problems during the development of Cusack Park provided source material for a heckling episode. A heckler suggested that Cowan was 'responsible for the spilling of blood' during the park's construction. 'The type of man who asked that question was the type of man who approved of Mr Kennedy's glorification of Hitler' was how Cowan responded to that claim. He explained that he joined the Labour Party to end the dominance of money over policy and to ensure that government was used for the benefit of the people. There was no fundamental difference between Fianna Fáil and Fine Gael: 'The two big parties always worked together when it was a question of trampling on the interests of the ordinary people. Labour appealed to the intelligent people of the country to vote for them. The fools could vote for de Valera.'[9] A similar message was delivered at Slane. The two main parties were 'more concerned with reducing income tax for the benefit of financiers than with looking after the interests of the labourers.' Labour Party policy insisted that the wealth of these financiers should be used for the benefit of the country as a whole. Cowan believed these financiers were responsible for a whispering campaign that suggested that the Labour Party was communistic. Cowan publicly rejected this idea: 'I am no Communist' he declared, 'nor would I be associated with a Communist party, because Communism is a degradation of the worker'. The people of Ireland were Christian and the Labour Party 'would be with the people of this country if there was any attack on their religion from outside'.[10] The workers' republic constitution had attracted the attention of the Catholic hierarchy and had raised alarm bells within Church circles. The hierarchy began to display a preoccupation with the dangers of communism in Ireland, especially in Lenten pastorals, and various newspapers including the *Limerick Leader*, the *Catholic Standard*, the *Irish Rosary* and the *Irish Catholic* all expressed concern that their new constitution placed the Labour Party on a slippery road towards communism.[11]

Cowan's appeal to the voters' intelligence made little impact and the electorate of the five-seat Meath–Westmeath constituency returned three Fianna Fáil and two Fine Gael candidates to the Dáil. Cowan's 2,160 first preference votes, 4.49 per cent of the total valid poll, placed him in eighth place in the field of eleven candidates, and behind the four Fianna Fáil and three Fine Gael candidates. He reportedly received 'fair support in Meath, though the support accorded him in Navan was not up to expectations'. He received 737 of John Hayden's transfers and 222 transfers from the surplus of the Fine Gael candidate, Capt. Patrick Giles. His final tally of 3,253 votes was well short of the quota of 8,020.[12] In a post-election analysis, Cowan identified the short time at his disposal for building an effective election machine and the lack of a strong branch network as the greatest handicaps he faced. The practice whereby the candidate was expected to provide all the finances to fund an election campaign would also have to be ended. It was important that local branches establish a fund to meet local expenses and in the long-term branches needed to be in a position to finance all campaign expenses.[13] With these issues in mind and in anticipation of an early general election in 1938, Cowan returned to Westmeath in October 1937 and addressed open air rallies in the eastern half of the county in Mullingar and Kinnegad. He established a new branch in Castlepollard and arrangements were made to set up branches in Coole and Whitehall. Addressing the crowds after Sunday Mass was the standard practice of the time and was often followed by the formation of a party branch. After such an address in January 1938, a branch was formed in Ballivor, Co. Meath.[14] In November, an address to the electorate of the constituency was issued by the party on behalf of Cowan and his running-mate John Hayden that outlined the twenty-points policy of the party and Cowan addressed a major rally in Mullingar where party policy was explained.[15] The snap general election was held on 17 June 1938. The signing of the Anglo-Irish Agreement on 25 April 1938 was a significant diplomatic triumph for Eamon de Valera and the Fianna Fáil administration. British control over the 'Treaty Ports' of Cobh, Bearhaven and Lough Swilly was ended as was the claim to naval and military facilities at these ports. The Economic War was ended with the agreement that Ireland would pay £10 million as a final financial settlement of all points of issue between Ireland and Britain including the British claim to payment of land annuities.[16] A month later de Valera travelled to Limerick to attend the funeral of his uncle Pat Coll. In his absence, the government was defeated by a single vote on a private member's bill calling for mandatory arbitration in disputes between the government and civil servants. Sixteen Fianna Fáil TDs missed the vote, which prompted the suspicion that some were encouraged to absent themselves to create the opportunity for a snap election. An immediate general election was announced with 17 June chosen as the polling date.[17]

Peadar Cowan launched his campaign in Navan and focussed on the local and the international in his inaugural address. He claimed that the government had trampled on the Fianna Fáil organization in Meath during the year and warned that in Russia, Germany and Italy, three countries with strong governments, 'individual freedom was a thing of the past'. 'Éire had fought bitterly for its freedom, and should be slow to take a chance of losing the personal liberty of the citizens ... Freedom was at stake in this election and the people should not lose sight of that fact on polling day'.[18] On 1 June, he addressed a public rally in the Market Square, Mullingar. There were no lies too bad to be told about him, he told the gathering: he was called a communist and a Blueshirt, he had introduced scab labour to Mullingar and he had lowered the conditions of working people. He warned that Eamon de Valera's desire for a strong government endangered democracy. 'This was supposed to be a democratic country but government by one man was not democratic'. The Labour Party policy and programme promised first and foremost 'a living wage for every worker in the country and for those people who cannot get work we stand definitely for sufficient maintenance to enable them and their families to live in comfort'. Conscious that he was speaking in a town with a large army barracks, Cowan highlighted the fact that as part of the Anglo-Irish agreement £600,000 was to be invested in up-grading obsolete ports 'which may involve this country in a murderous war with some foreign power' at a time when 'we have soldiers serving in the army, married men, who are paid 17s. 6d. a week'. There was no money available to provide schemes of work for unemployed people yet the government was able to raise £10 million to pay the British for the ending of the Economic War.[19] Later in the month, on 12 June, Cowan addressed rallies at Trim where St Patrick's Pipe Band played before and after the rally and at Kildalkey.[20] He concluded his campaign with a tour of south Westmeath; in Kilbeggan he focussed on the necessity of providing free primary, secondary, vocational and university education with free books in 'order to have the best brains developed and used for the public good'; in Moate the focus was on the need for large-scale public works such as developing new roads fit for modern traffic, land drainage, housing, developing sewerage schemes and waterworks to create employment so that 'the shadow of hunger and misery would be driven from many homes'; in Kinnegad, agriculture topped the agenda. The remedies successfully introduced in New Zealand by the Labour Party would be introduced in Ireland. Farmers would be guaranteed both a price and a market for their produce. The ravages of the Economic War could only be ended by providing long-term, low-interest loans to farmers to enable them to reconstruct their farms; arbitration for civil servants in dispute with the government was also guaranteed; at Killalon, Cowan returned to the theme of adequate wages for workers, defined 'as one sufficient to maintain a man, his wife and average family under reasonable conditions of comfort'; in Athboy, the appeal was to members of the Old IRA who were dissatisfied with the decisions of the Pensions Board. As a member of the IRA, in the pre-Treaty days, 'imprisoned for a long period by the British authorities', Peadar Cowan promised to press for an amendment to the Act to 'provide for more generous treatment for men who served in the lower ranks in the struggle'; at fair day in Clonmellon the 'tyrannical manner in which the Fianna Fáil organization in Meath was treated by a minister since the last general election' was central to his address. The organization was 'threatened, bullied and insulted and this showed the danger of giving any political party power to act in such tyrannical fashion'. The claims of the local farmers must get first preference in the division of land; it was natural that young men should seek to be established in their home neighbourhood.[21] These references to the treatment of the farmers in Meath related to the government scheme that was introduced in the mid-1930s acting on a recommendation in the Gaeltacht Commission Report published in 1927. An area of 776 acres was obtained by the Land Commission in Rath Cairn, Co. Meath, and in March 1935, 27 Irish-speaking natives of Connemara were settled in new houses in fully equipped farms. Two more Gaeltacht colonies were established soon after in Gibstown and Kilbride. The scheme fitted the Fianna Fáil party policy of promoting land redistribution and the revival of the Irish language.

Cowan was the lone Labour Party candidate contesting the Meath–Westmeath constituency on this occasion along with three Fianna Fáil and three Fine Gael candidates in a constituency that attracted a 79.4 per cent turnout of eligible voters. He faced an impossible task as he was joined on the ballot paper by the five outgoing TDs and Michael Sweeney, a third Fine Gael member contesting the seat. Cowan polled 4,621 first preference votes, a remarkable achievement and an increase of 114 per cent on his 1937 total and 9.5 per cent of the total valid poll. This was not enough to get elected and he was eliminated after the fourth count, his final total of 5,305 votes was 3,100 behind Capt. Patrick Giles, the fifth candidate elected.[22]

In 1942, Cowan became the Director of Organization of the Labour Party during which time the number of branches expanded rapidly increasing from 174 in 1941 to 750 in 1943, a growth that was reflected in the return of seventeen Labour TDs in the general election of 1943. One of these branches was established in Rathowen, Co. Westmeath, on 8 February 1942 when Cowan addressed an after-Mass meeting.[23] Cowan faced the electorate in the Meath–Westmeath constituency for the third time. On this occasion Cowan and his two Labour Party running mates, John Fitzgerald and Charles McGurk, began their campaign early and were on the campaign trail in February and March.[24] Cowan and Fitzgerald were selected at a constituency convention held in Navan on 24 January and McGurk was selected in Mullingar, a week later. The selection of Fitzgerald overturned a previous decision made in Athboy in which Seán Doyle was selected. Doyle subsequently resigned from the party and contested the election as a Republican Labour candidate.[25] On 25 January at Meath-Hill and on 21 February at after-Mass meetings at Kentstown, Co. Meath, Peadar Cowan delivered a detailed outline of what he called the Labour Party's 'practical and constructive programme to uplift the workers and to give them a decent standard of comfort and security'. The policy was based on 'the practical application of the encyclicals of Popes Leo XIII and Pius XI'. The keystone of the policy was the promise of a guaranteed minimum wage of £3 per week to all workers, the minimum required to provide the 'bare necessities of life for a man, his wife and three children'. The policy also included a promise to pay a family allowance of 5s. per week to each child 'after the third' under 16 years of age and to increase the old age pension to £1 per week to be paid at 65 years of age. An increase was also promised to widows and orphans in receipt of pensions. The policy had a definite purpose: 'the building up of the family and the guarantee of the workers and their families of purchasing power'. This, in turn, would stimulate the economy and provide a guaranteed market for farmers and manufacturers. The agricultural policy also involved strict control of middlemen such as bacon curers and flour millers who were making 'huge profits', thus the increased prices to the farmers would not result in an increased cost of living. The Labour Party also planned to create job opportunities in state sponsored schemes for the unemployed, with a guaranteed weekly wage of £3, in afforestation, land reclamation, drainage, bog development, turf production and road maintenance. These initiatives were possible, it was claimed, without any increase in taxation by 'government control of our own financial system and utilization of Irish credit in Irish interests'. It was essential to break the stranglehold of the British financial system to ensure that the volume of credit necessary to pay the workers engaged in the 'constructive national work' was available.[26] This message was repeated across the constituency. In Trim, on 6 May 1943, Cowan relayed the party's opposition to the internment of Irish citizens without trial and promised that the party, on coming to power, would immediately release every Irish citizen so imprisoned. 'Freedom of opinion and freedom of speech are fundamental of Labour party policy'.[27] The meeting staged at Ballinagore was reportedly the largest every held in the Westmeath village and continued well past midnight. Westmeath was the county 'where he spent so many years in happy association with the Gaels of the county in doing work in which they all took a just pride'. Re-electing the present government would be a 'national tragedy'. 'There is no difference between Fianna Fáil and Fine Gael, except some personal differences between the party leaders'. Under both regimes Irish people experienced 'hunger and destitution and want on the one hand, and big salaries and extravagant pensions for the privileged on the other'. Money was available to pay ministerial annual salaries of £1,000 and Mr de Valera's salary of £2,500, money was available to fight war and it was essential that plenty of money was found 'to fight the war against hunger, poverty and destitution'. Cowan promised that the party would secure the necessary finance without increasing taxes or rates 'by breaking the financial link with England, establishing our own monetary institution and creating the credit necessary to pay the £3 a week to the men put on the great State scheme mentioned'.[28] Cowan completed his campaign with rallies at Clonard, Ballivor, Kinnegad and Coralstown where he promised an end to 'rotational employment and no more slave wages'. The Labour Party 'believed in political independence, which enabled the people to seek economic and social security, to develop the resources of the country, to keep the people at home and provide them with useful work, and to raise the standard of living and comfort for all sections of the population'.[29] In his role as Director of Organization, he also addressed the electorate in other constituencies. In late January, he addressed public meetings at Castlebar, Westport and Claremorris; on 18 and 19 June, he addressed rallies at Donegal, Ballyshannon and Sligo.[30]

Fourteen candidates faced the electorate in the Meath–Westmeath constituency on 22 June and Cowan's 3,983 first preference vote, 8.26 per cent of the votes cast, was the fourth highest in the constituency but the combined Labour vote was still short of a quota. Despite doing well from the transfers of McGurk and Fitzgerald and from Joseph Cooney (Clann na Talmhan), he was eliminated at the eleventh count with the outgoing Fianna Fáil deputies M.J. Kennedy and Matthew O'Reilly claiming the last two seats without reaching the quota. O'Reilly finished just 302 votes ahead of Cowan. The division in the party had some impact and Cowan fared relatively poorly from Seán Doyle's transfers.[31] The results were unsatisfactory from the perspective of Eamon de Valera and Fianna Fáil; the governing party lost ten seats although there was consolation in the fact the Fine Gael results were worse. The main opposition party returned with 32 seats, a loss of 13 since 1938. The Labour Party won eight additional seats and returned 17 TDs to the 11th Dáil. The new farmers' party Clann na Talmhan was the big winner with 10 TDs; four independent farmer TDs were also elected, along with eight independents. Eamon de Valera had failed to get the majority he sought. When the new Dáil convened he was re-elected Taoiseach as both the Labour Party and Clann na Talmhan opted not to oppose de Valera on the basis that he was the leader of the largest party.[32]

These were troubled years for the Labour Party as it struggled with its radical left members. The 'workers' republic' constitution of 1936 and its commitment to a workers' republic was removed at the party's annual conference in April 1939 and this ended the party's last tentative commitment to socialism until the 1960s.[33] The constitution was abandoned after the Irish National Teachers' Organization (INTO) received clarification from the hierarchy that it was in conflict with Catholic social teaching. In the words of Niamh Puirséil, 'the right-wing press and the Catholic Church were infinitely stronger than the Left inside or outside the Labour [Party]'.[34] Dropping the socialist clauses from the constitution did not provoke a mass exodus from the party; in fact the opposite happened. During the course of the Emergency, the Labour Party became a magnet for radicals of many hues. In 1941, the USSR entered the Second World War on the side of the Allies and rather than support Britain, the Communist Party of Ireland (CPI) disbanded in July. The party continued in Northern Ireland but the southern members were instructed to join the Labour Party. Big Jim Larkin returned to the party much to the chagrin of his arch enemy, William O'Brien, and others of the Irish Transport and General Workers' Union (ITGWU) leadership who threatened to disaffiliate from the party if Larkin's membership was not cancelled. As Director of Organization, Peadar Cowan's recommendation that the party in 'Dublin city and Townships' be placed under the control of an executive committee composed of three representatives from each of the area's four constituency councils was approved by the Administrative Council and implemented. Cowan presided when the committee's officers were appointed. James Larkin junior was appointed chairman, E. O'Sullivan vice-chairman, John Ireland was appointed secretary and M.J. Gaffney, treasurer.[35] Both Larkin junior and Ireland were enthusiastic communists. Not alone was Jim Larkin's (senior) membership accepted, he was nominated as a Labour Party candidate in the Dublin North-East constituency and was elected to Dáil Éireann in 1943.

In January 1944, the ITGWU disaffiliated from the Labour Party and the split was sealed when five of its TD members formed the National Labour Party. To camouflage the vindictive root of the split, O'Brien claimed that his real concern lay with communist infiltration of the party, a claim echoed by the five departed deputies. William Norton was challenged to accept an investigation by 'the bishops or any impartial body'. O'Brien added a second coat of camouflage by cooperating with the Catholic newspaper the *Standard* in promoting an anti-communist witch-hunt by publishing a series of articles on communism in the Labour Party.[36] O'Brien was supported by academics such as Professor Alfred O'Rahilly, the president of University College Cork, who contributed at length to the *Standard* features. In January 1944, O'Brien, the general secretary of the ITGWU, in a circular letter sent to each branch of the ITGWU, charged 'a majority of the Administrative Council' of the Labour Party with having 'allowed and encouraged admission into the Party of people who have been active members of and well known propagandists for the Communist Party'. O'Rahilly, as 'a friend of Labour', feared that any flirtation with communism 'will inevitably produce in this country a vigorous reaction which will reduce Labour to political impotence'. The time for a showdown was long overdue.[37] Peadar Cowan enthusiastically engaged in the discourse. As a Catholic, he found the 'malicious attacks on the Labour Party' of the articles 'painful and offensive' as they were 'to thousands of other Catholics in the Labour Party'. 'It is time to talk bluntly' he pointed out.

> In matters of religion, Catholics take their guidance and directions from the Church and they resent abuse, vilification and patronising fulminations from sanctimonious political humbugs who seem to think that they can do the Bishops' work better than the Bishops and have no scruples or hesitation in using a cloak of religion for their own political purposes.

The Labour Party was not going to allow a union executive dictate to it as to who or who should not be a member and was not going to 'tolerate totalitarian or any other form of despotism either naked or disguised'.[38] William Norton opted for an internal inquiry and as a result of this investigation six members were expelled, the Liam Mellows branch in Cork was dissolved as was the party's central branch and the Dublin executive. From this point onwards, radical Labour Party members exercised caution and were careful not to say anything that was likely to cause offence. In practical terms, this meant that any mention of socialism was forbidden and anything that could be interpreted as critical of the Catholic Church was avoided at all costs. The Labour Party was no longer an attractive home for radicals. Pragmatism was William Norton's guiding principle and as Niamh Purséil has noted anything that was likely to cost the party votes was strictly off limits, 'whether it was socialism, criticism of the Church or supporting republicans in Spain – Norton would always walk away'.[39]

Those of a radical disposition justified their position by citing papal encyclicals and Catholic social teaching in their election speeches and in their newspaper responses to the attacks of their political opponents. This was the only way to attack capitalism without being tagged a communist. Peadar Cowan used this technique on a regular basis. Shortly after the 1938 general election, Cowan informed the readers of the *Meath Chronicle* of the contents of a lecture he attended in the Mansion House entitled 'The Future of the Catholic Home in Ireland' delivered by Dr Michael Browne, bishop of Galway. In this lecture, which 'seemed an echo from the speeches made on my platforms during the recent election campaigns', Browne stated that when 'public opinion was educated to the importance of Christian homes then it would be possible for the democratic State to make some gravely needed social and economic changes which were necessary for the encouragement of Christian homes'. The provision of decent housing was the first requirement and 'great progress' had been made in that direction according to Browne; 'the removal of unemployment among men and the provision of employment or land for young men at a decent wage was the next essential'. A long-term plan of reconstruction, agreed by all parties, was needed to end the 'moral cancer of unemployment', one that would continue regardless of what party was in power. Cowan ended the letter by suggesting that 'everything else ought to be subordinated to one great effort to abolish unemployment and increase wages for the large number of workers who are scandalously underpaid'.[40] The government that determined to do these things was guaranteed 'the support of every man and woman of goodwill in the state'. The *Drogheda Independent* also published a letter from Cowan in which he quoted from Pope Leo XIII's encyclical *Rerum Novarum* to again establish his Catholic credentials (fig. 2). According to the encyclical, justice demands 'that the interests of the working classes should be carefully watched over by the administration so that those who contribute so largely to the advantage of the community may themselves share in the benefits in which they create – that being housed, clothed and bodily fit they may find their life less hard and more endurable'.[41] In his 1943 election campaign, Cowan made constant reference to

> During the election campaign I spoke often of the duty of the State to see that the interests of all workers are properly looked after and in this connection I can do no better than quote the words of His Holiness Pope Leo XIII in "Rerum Novarum."
>
> "It may be truly said that it is only by the labour of workingmen that States grow rich. Justice therefore demands that the interests of the working classes should be carefully watched over by the administration so that those who contribute so largely to the advantage of the community may themselves share in the benefits which they create—that being housed, clothed, and bodily fit they may find their life less hard and more endurable."
>
> Yours faithfully,
> PEADAR COWAN.

2. Extract from Peadar Cowan's letter to *Drogheda Independent*, 2 July 1938.

the teachings of Popes Leo XIII and Pius XI and the importance of creating a society that would enable a family to live in 'frugal comfort'.[42]

Eamon de Valera returned to the country at the first opportunity in search of an overall majority. Both Fine Gael and the Labour Party were in crisis. W.T. Cosgrave had retired as leader of Fine Gael and his successor Richard Mulcahy had lost his seat in the 1943 election and exercised his leadership from the Senate. On 9 May 1944, the government was defeated by a single vote on the Transport Bill and Eamon de Valera made the journey to Áras an Uachtaráin and requested the President, Douglas Hyde, to dissolve the Dáil. Hyde agreed but under emergency legislation the outgoing Dáil remained in existence until its successor was elected.[43] The 1944 election campaign was short and swift with the Labour Party attempting to portray the election as an attempt by Fianna Fáil to achieve de Valera's wish for a one-man one-party government. 'He wanted, in effect to be the bridegroom at a wedding, the baby at the Christening and the remains at the funeral'.[44] For the fourth time, Peadar Cowan was a candidate in the Meath–Westmeath constituency and began his campaign in Mullingar by claiming that the election was pre-planned to enable de Valera and Fianna Fáil achieve its objective of one-man, one-party government. 'The decision to advise dissolution was taken long before the Transport Bill was introduced as well as the decision to hold the election before June 1 which would deprive the young men and women of their vote'.[45] A series of Labour Party meetings were held across the constituency on Sunday 21 May with Cowan addressing those assembled at Kilbeg and Staholmog after opening the campaign in Trim where he claimed the election was called with the intention of 'wiping out the Labour Party and Clann na Talmhan so that Fianna Fáil could again achieve an all-clear majority', an ominous development 'for the people who do not forget the five year dictatorship of a Fianna Fáil majority until that majority was wiped out by an exasperated electorate less than a year ago'. He concluded his campaign with a public meeting at the Market Square in Navan on 27 May 1944 where Big Jim Larkin was the lead speaker. Earlier in the day, Larkin and Cowan addressed the electorate at Dunshaughlin.[46] Cowan retained his vote, polling 3,961 first preference votes (9 per cent of the valid poll) but the election was a triumph for the Fianna Fáil candidate Michael Hilliard who was elected on the first count with a surplus of 1,271 votes. A year earlier Hilliard was elected on the eighth count without reaching the quota.[47] The Hilliard vote was a reflection of national trends. Fianna Fáil finished 29 percentage points ahead of its nearest rival, a gap never seen before or since. The Labour Party won eight seats, and the National Labour Party four, a loss of five seats on the united Labour performance of the previous year.[48]

PEADAR COWAN OPTS FOR SOCIALISM: THE VANGUARD

Peadar Cowan resigned from the Labour Party shortly afterwards and established The Vanguard. The intention was to provide a welcoming home for radicals and to keep the socialist agenda as part of the political discourse of the Labour Party. In pursuing this agenda, Cowan provided his political opponents with a stick to beat him with for the remainder of his political career. According to The Vanguard manifesto, issued by Cowan on 20 August 1944, the movement took its 'inspiration and guidance from the teachings of our patriot leaders – Tone, Emmet, Lalor, Davitt, Connolly, Pearse and Mellows' and was founded for 'the express purpose of creating the situation that will end capitalism in Ireland, establish a socialist republic for all Ireland and undo the British conquest in all its phases, political, cultural and economic'. The manifesto's opening paragraphs painted a depressing picture of the Ireland of the day where 'the prevalence of unemployment, poverty, hunger, corruption in its various forms, racketeering, profiteering, licentiousness and crime is a serious and dangerous threat to the nation'. It was 'pitiable to see hunger and misery in thousands of Irish homes' in a country where 'The plight of the unemployed, of the sick, the maimed, the blind and of the widow, the orphan, the infirm and the old age pensioner is beyond the power of words adequately to describe.' Tuberculosis and other diseases were taking their daily toll on men, women and children too weakened by hunger to fight the diseases. This situation existed while 'a small minority lived in luxury, controlling the whole financial and industrial mechanism of the State and enslaving the great majority of decent honest hardworking men and women by virtue of their financial power and the despotic economic domination they are permitted to exercise over their fellow citizens'. The state was run in the interests of this 'small, privileged and unprincipled minority whilst the common people are forcibly kept on and below the level of starvation'. This was a product of the Cosgrave and de Valera administrations who were 'content to remain the instruments of the rotten discredited and criminal capitalist system'. It was claimed that the termination of hostilities with Britain will lead to the formation of a league or Federation of European Socialist Republics and as a socialist republic Ireland will have 'the power to break the political connection with the British Empire, and abolish Partition'. There was only one hope for the Irish people. 'Capitalism, the cause of all our social evils, must be destroyed, and with it, its agents, the financiers, racketeers, profiteers, and landlords who are the enemies of the common people'. And as a means of achieving this objective, The Vanguard would operate a system of democratic centralism, which required that every member obeyed the instructions of the leaders.[49]

Cowan elaborated on the intentions of the new organization at a number of public meetings held in Dublin. On 22 September, in the Engineers' Hall in Dawson Street, Dublin, he explained that it was not intended to form a new party but by propaganda and activity in Labour Party branches and elsewhere 'to lead the working classes and the working farmers to a socialist republic'. The crisis in the Labour Party in which the party was attacked from both inside and outside had succeed because the rank-and-file members did not understand the foundations on which the party was established by James Connolly. Members were expelled at the behest of a secret religious organization, the Knights of Columbanus, 'the most dangerous organization' in the state. 'These people are so powerful, that they control all the senior appointments in the state and they control the political parties. One of the functions of this new organization will be to get hold of this secret religious organization and destroy it'.[50] In an address to the Amalgamated Upholsterers' Union, he explained that the purpose of Vanguard was to unite the labour movement on the basis of socialism and to take advantage of the 'favourable world situation to establish an Irish Socialist Republic'.[51] At the Dublin University Fabian Society, he explained that the capitalist system was responsible for most of the evils of the world and true progress was only possible under a system of socialism and 'instead of tinkering with capitalism we should take the bold step of abolishing it and replacing it by socialism'.[52] James Everett, the leader of the National Labour Party, took advantage of Cowan's initiative and availed of the opportunity to attack the Labour Party: 'the new communist organization – The Vanguard' showed how helplessly the leaders were caught 'in the communist web'. The leaders of The Vanguard were those who 'crashed' the Labour Party in 1942, founded the 'notorious' Dublin Central Branch and caused the party constitution to be torn up.[53] William Norton acted swiftly and the Labour Party quickly distanced itself from Cowan's movement and announced that he had resigned from the party in August 1944. Party branches were informed that the party had no responsibility for the Vanguard or the 'utterances of Cowan or those associated with him'.[54] The Vanguard movement did not survive for long and in October 1945, Cowan re-joined the Fairview branch of the Labour Party before he resigned again in July 1946 to join Clann na Poblachta.[55] Prior to leaving, he made one more visit to his old Westmeath stomping ground and addressed a party rally in Athlone where his socialist principles were again unveiled. The future of the Athlone Woollen Mills was topical at the time and the concern was cited by Cowan as an example of an essential industry that should not be controlled by private individuals but as one that should be maintained for the interests of the community. He insisted that it was a disgrace that it had not been rebuilt despite its central importance to the interests of the people.[56] The factory, which employed between 400 and 500 people and was central to the economy of the town, was destroyed by fire in November 1940.

Cowan's association with the Labour Party ended shortly afterwards. Clann na Poblachta was apparently a more suitable vehicle for his radical social principles and his strong nationalist position. He was unable to break the Fianna Fáil–Fine Gael stranglehold in the five seat constituency but succeeded in increasing his personal vote from 2,160 first preferences in 1937 to 4,621 in 1938 and he polled just over 3,900 votes in the 1943 and 1944 elections. The police reports credit Cowan with putting 'a tremendous amount of work and energy into his labour activities' but suggest that he was never fully accepted 'as a genuine worker in labour interests by some of the prominent labour leaders because of the feeling that he was using their party as a means to an end' and was disadvantaged by his lack of a union background.[57]

3. Peadar Cowan and Clann na Poblachta

THE REPUBLICAN PRISONERS' RELEASE ASSOCIATION (RPRA)

During the second World War, members of the IRA were treated to the full rigours of the law. In January 1939 a legal loophole was closed and legislation that allowed the internment without trial of Irish citizens was introduced and was deemed constitutional by the Supreme Court on 9 February.[1] At one stage there were approximately 450 men, all members of the IRA, in various internment camps and prisons, as well as a large number who were sent to prison by the Special Criminal Court.[2] Six IRA men were executed and three veterans of the republican struggle were allowed to die on hunger strike.[3] Hunger strikes were used by IRA prisoners as a protest and to leverage their release. Much of this was hidden from the Irish public as the period was also a time of strict censorship. The lifting of wartime censorship and associated restrictions brought news of political prisoners into the public domain and was to have a significant political impact. Rumours about the conditions of prisoners held in Portlaoise became rooted in fact and towards the end of 1945, the Republican Prisoners' Release Association (RPRA) was formed in Dublin. According to the RPRA constitution issued in April 'The Association has no connection with any political party, and its appeal is directed to all freedom-loving men and women who believe in the right of Ireland to be free from foreign aggression in any form'.[4]

Peadar Cowan was one of the leading personalities in the RPRA. In the months of May and June, he traversed the country speaking on its behalf, appearing on public platforms in Dublin, Portlaoise, Carrick-on-Suir, Clonmel, Callan, Cashel, Thurles, Tipperary, Waterford, Galway, Athenry, Tuam, Loughrea, Ballinrobe and Navan where calls were made for the release of all political prisoners held in Éire, Northern Ireland and Great Britain and for an enquiry into conditions in Portlaoise Prison.[5] In Navan, Cowan addressed what he termed 'one of the worst and most disgraceful tragedies to happen in this country ... which had brought a blush of shame on the people as a whole'. He was referring to the death of Seán McCaughey in Portlaoise Prison, 'a young Belfast man and a member of the IRA' who was brought before the Military Tribunal on what Cowan termed 'a minor charge of assault'.[6] McCaughey was involved in the prolonged interrogation of IRA Chief of Staff Seán Hayes who was subjected to an IRA court martial and held under house arrest on suspicion of being a police informer. Hayes escaped from his captors and when he surrendered to the police he was carrying a revolver and wearing the remains of chains and ropes with which he had been bound. He was sentenced to five years imprisonment in June 1942.[7] During McCaughey's trial, Hayes gave evidence of his beatings and torture by his IRA captors. McCaughey was charged with the possession of incriminating documents and ammunition without a licence and sentenced to death by firing squad which was later commuted to life imprisonment.[8] When he went to Portlaoise, Cowan explained, 'following the traditions of all members of the IRA and according to the traditions of the Fenians and nationalists, he refused to wear convicts' garb'. McCaughey entered Portlaoise Prison on 24 July 1940 and from then until the autumn of 1944 he was wrapped in a prison blanket, kept in solitary confinement and deprived of exercise and fresh air. When the war ended, in May 1945, many internees were released but convicted IRA prisoners remained in prison. McCaughey began a hunger strike on 19 April and he died on 11 May. In the same month, the North of Ireland executive to the embarrassment of the de Valera administration unconditionally released David Fleming, a Kerry native who had also been on hunger strike. The McCaughey family were represented by Seán MacBride, Noel Hartnett and Con Lehane at the inquest and during his cross examination of the prison doctor, MacBride extracted an admission from the doctor that he would not treat a dog in the manner in which McCaughey had been treated. As a tribute to McCaughey, Cowan, still a member of the Labour Party, called on the electorate of Meath 'to say that the government and the men who tortured Seán McCaughey would no longer be tolerated by them and when they had the opportunity in the near future to remove them from power for ever … and put an end to the regime of cruelty uncompared to anywhere in the civilized world'.[9] At a rally in Waterford, Cowan claimed that the reaction of the people to the news of McCaughey's death would spell disaster for Fianna Fáil at the next general election. The death was 'a blow to Fianna Fáil from which it can never recover. Fianna Fáil like other political parties of the past, was passing into oblivion'. The Irish people abhorred anything that savoured of injustice, unfair play or cruelty and the jury's verdict at the inquest had disturbed public opinion. Censorship had been abused and had prevented people from knowing what was being done in their name. 'The lifting of the censorship had exposed terrible conditions to the public gaze, and the totalitarian activities of the government and individual ministers could no longer be concealed, and would be tolerated no longer'.[10] In an emotional address at Cashel, Cowan asked

> Who among this audience, father or mother, boy or girl, would like to see a son or brother, locked up in a small cell for four-and-a half-years, without clothes for those four-and-a half-years, without seeing the sunlight except what might percolate through prison bars; without seeing a human being except the warder; without having clothes winter or summer, except the blanket that covered his bed, without a boot to protect his feet from the

cold stone floor of his cell, without a sock or a shirt, without any covering except the blanket wrapped around him. How would you like your boy or your brother to be treated in that way? Seán McCaughey was a fine type of young Irishman. He was six feet in height, broad-shouldered. When he left Portlaoise Prison, there came nothing but a few bones, covered with red skin, that any boy in this audience could carry.[11]

THE FORMATION OF CLANN NA POBLACHTA

On Thursday 6 June 1947, Cowan, Noel Hartnett, Con Lehane, Roger McHugh, Seán Óg O'Tuama, Seán O'Grady and Paud O'Donoghue addressed a meeting held at the Mansion House, Dublin.[12] Noel Hartnett, a former member of the Fianna Fáil Árd-Chomhairle, was banned from acting as a radio host by the Minister for Posts and Telegraph, P.J. Little, for his role in the RPRA.[13] A month later these key members of the RPRA formed the nucleus of those who established a new political party, Clann na Poblachta, with Seán MacBride as leader. In MacBride's memoir, he 'concretely' remembers having 'several talks with Con Lehane, Noel Hartnett, and Captain Peadar Cowan as he was then' about the formation of a political party 'that would have its purpose as the bringing about of a change of government'.[14] All four were members of the legal profession and the preliminary talks generally took place in the Law Library, usually in the evening after court. Cowan, as a former member of the army of the Irish Free State, 'brought a completely new element into republican circles in that he was prepared to join in order to bring about change and the adoption of a more progressive policy by Irish governments', according to MacBride.[15] Involvement with the RPRA was not the only formal association of the core group of individuals who established Clann na Poblachta. Many were members of the cross-party Irish Republican Army Old Comrades Association set up in 1943; Seán MacBride was chairman of this body, Dónal O'Donoghue was secretary and Cowan and Con Lehane were executive members. In March 1943, the organization's national executive passed a resolution calling for the staging of a national convention to consider the best means of bringing about the restoration of the de facto Republic for the whole of Ireland, free from any outside influence.[16]

The founding meeting of Clann na Poblachta was held in Barry's Hotel, Dublin, on 6 July 1946 at which it was made clear that the party planned to contest elections and enter the Dáil. A short statement was issued, the signatories were constituted as the provisional executive, and it was planned to hold an Ard Fheis to formulate a detailed programme and adopt a constitution. The new party placed considerable emphasis on ending partition but also focused on living conditions. The statement referenced the forced migration of Irish youth, unemployment, low wages and the rising cost of living for workers while a small section of the Irish public was enabled to accumulate enormous wealth. A strong political party was needed to end these evils and the system that created them and 'to set up an ideal before the nation and a new standard of political morality in public life'. The *Irish Times* reported that the new party meant that a 'very large section of what you might call the IRA' are taking constitutional action.[17] At least twenty-two out of the provisional executive of twenty-seven had been active in the IRA at some stage of their lives.[18]

Clann na Poblachta attracted those disillusioned by Fianna Fáil's perceived movement away from republicanism and the widespread imprisonment of republicans. It also attracted political novices such as Noël Browne who were interested in social reform. Cowan and Noel Hartnett brought to the table essential political capital that MacBride and other members lacked. Cowan in particular, as we have seen, had over a decade of engagement with party politics at grass-roots level and of administration at national executive level, and of contesting elections as well as possessing tremendous organizational ability. He became the party's director of finance. Cowan and Hartnett played a central role in selecting candidates and establishing constituency organizations to contest the three by-elections of 1947 and the 1948 general election. However, as Eithne MacDermott has pointed out, they were also men who enjoyed influence without power within the party, which posed difficulties for both men when they fell out with the party leader.[19] The existence of what Seán MacBride calls a 'type of clannishness among older republicans' in the party meant that Noel Hartnett and Noël Browne, who were never in the IRA or active in the republican movement, were treated differently to old republicans. Peadar Cowan was in a similar situation and in MacBride's words 'was regarded as purely a Free State army officer by some of my republican colleagues, who were rather alarmed to have him involved in Clann under any circumstances'.[20]

Like the other key figures in the party, Cowan went on tour explaining party policy and addressed by-election and general election rallies. Cowan, Seán MacBride and Noel Hartnett were the main travelling salesmen for the party. The trail began in Roscrea in March 1947 where Seán MacBride branded Clann na Poblachta as 'a truly independent and distinctive national organization pledged to reintegrate the whole of Ireland'. He called on young people to join the party as political life had become the monopoly of 'tired old men'. He was accompanied by Cowan on the platform. 'The farmers were the backbone of the country' Cowan explained in Thurles, and 'until agriculture was put on a sound footing there would be a continuous flight from the land'. Rural communities had been neglected and farm labourers were paid 'starvation wages'.[21] He told his audience at Newport, Co. Tipperary, that Fianna Fáil had failed to deliver on its promises and had 'acted in absolute opposition' to the policies it had promoted. The party was the enemy of the workers and every time workers attempted to improve their 'wages or conditions, their greatest enemy was the Fianna Fáil government'. Fianna Fáil had done nothing practical to end partition and its incompetence was responsible for the 'dreadful drain of emigration that has bled this country white'. It was 'a fundamental necessity that Fianna Fáil be wiped out of political existence at the earliest possible moment'. Clann na Poblachta promised a policy of putting the unemployed to work on schemes of national reconstruction that included afforestation, slum clearance, house building and road modernization. 'Every unemployed person could be employed on these national works and would be so employed by Clann na Poblachta', and paid a living wage or 'a wage sufficient to enable an adult to marry and raise a family in reasonable comfort'. It was essential that wages and the cost of living were linked. Instead of 'doles and vouchers', Clann na Poblachta proposed to give work 'at a decent minimum wage based on the actual cost of living'. The required finances would be created by the Central Bank 'freed from the present entanglement with sterling'. The party also had good news for the farming community. 'Economic prices and a market for everything the farmer had to sell' was promised. This would enable a farmer to pay his workers a living wage 'and make a comfortable and secure living for himself'. The profit-making opportunities of 'the big-middlemen' would be curtailed, which would ensure maximum profits for the producer and keep the cost to the consumer 'within reasonable bounds'.[22] The keystone of Clann na Poblachta's economic policy was full employment with guaranteed living wages, a policy that offered the only solution to the serious problems of emigration, hunger, disease and destitution, Cowan told his audience at Tallaght.

> We have important work waiting to be done – drainage, afforestation, road modernization, electrification of the railways, development of the bogs and production of electricity from turf, the building up of our fisheries and by-products, work that will provide employment, and give a valuable market to our farmers and factories.[23]

Only the most miserable social services were provided despite 'the stranglehold of taxes' and 'proved that a Christian order of society was impossible under Fianna Fáil … it is the fundamental duty of the electorate to ensure that is summarily and effectively dismissed at the next general election'.[24] In Holborn, Cowan addressed the London branch of the new party and branded Fianna Fáil 'the greatest enemy of republicanism ever known in Ireland'. Because Fianna Fáil members had deserted their ideals Clann na Poblachta was 'established to remove them from office'.[25] At Tubberclare, Co. Westmeath, he told his listeners that the problem of partition could be solved if conditions were made so good that 'their northern fellow countrymen would be attracted into a United Ireland'. The social services must be 'brought up to the standard of Northern Ireland'.[26] Peadar Cowan wrote that policies articulated ten years earlier, in a different context, by Bishop Browne of Galway 'seemed an echo from the speeches made on [his] platforms during the recent election campaigns'; now the social policies of Clann na Poblachta delivered by Cowan replicated almost exactly what he had delivered during his days as a candidate for election under the Labour Party banner.

SEÁN MAC ENTEE, PEADAR COWAN AND THE RED SCARE

As early as July 1947, the new party had attracted the attention of Seán MacEntee, the Minister for Local Government and Public Health in the Fianna Fáil administration, who warned the people not to be lured astray by the promises of Clann na Poblachta leaders whose past policies he strongly disagreed with. MacEntee had a accumulated a substantial portfolio of political assassination attempts at this stage. Despite supporting Fianna Fáil and Eamon de Valera in the vote for Taoiseach when the Dáil reassembled after the 1944 general election, Labour Party leader William Norton called for a Dáil division after de Valera announced an unchanged ministerial line-up, in protest against the inclusion of MacEntee, 'a specialist in throwing election muck'.[27] Peadar Cowan and Seán MacBride in particular were targeted in 1947. 'Do those subscribing to Clann na Poblachta approve of a movement of which Mr Peadar Cowan is one of the leaders and principal spokesmen, and are they prepared to accept Mr Peadar Cowan and his principles?' he asked those attending a Fianna Fáil anniversary function at Clery's Restaurant in Dublin on 12 July 1947, before wondering if Cowan and his associates were part of the vanguard of Clann na Poblachta or were the other Clann leaders part of the vanguard for Cowan.[28]

The by-elections in Dublin County, Tipperary and Waterford held on 29 October 1947 provided the first political test for the party and an early opportunity to measure the effectiveness of the nationwide publicity drive. Cowan called on the electorate to select better candidates instead of supporting 'voting machines who performed their parliamentary functions with their feet rather than with their brains'.[29] The results proved to be something of a political sensation as party leader Seán MacBride in Dublin and Patrick Kinnane in Tipperary won seats. The substantial transfers from Labour Party and Fine Gael candidates were instrumental in the successes and raised alarm bells in Fianna Fáil. Although there was a substantial drop in first preference votes, the Fianna Fáil candidates topped the poll in the three constituencies, but more than half the Labour Party transfers and 48 per cent of Fine Gael's transfers went to the Clann na Poblachta candidates.[30]

The first Ard Fheis of the party was held in Dublin on 30 November 1947 and was attended by 372 delegates representing 252 nationwide branches at which the party emphatically refuted the suggestion that it had 'Communistic, Fascist or unconstitutional tendencies' and declared that 'such widespread whispers and innuendos' were merely devices used by supporters of the Fianna Fáil party in an effort to maintain themselves in office (fig. 3).

Answer Please!

Clann Na Poblachta

1 WHAT DID MR. COWAN MEAN WHEN HE SAID:

    (a) "The world situation to-day is composed of four ideologies—Communism, Fascism, National Socialism and the Corporate State, and that the last three will disappear?"

    (b) "Socialism" (i.e., Communism) "is the next development due in this country. . . . It will only be achieved by uprising and a revolutionary movement of workers and working farmers?"

                                               ("Standard," 29/9/'44.)

2 Did not "The Standard" describe Mr. Cowan as "this homemade Lenin," and say (29/9/'44):

    "What Mr. Cowan is attempting to launch is, in fact, a Communist organisation. . . . The manifesto . . . is a programme of class war, confiscation and State-control."

3. Fianna Fáil election advertisement targeting Peadar Cowan (*Irish Press*, 2 Feb. 1948).

The party's provisional policy was formally adopted and the fundamental principles of the party were defined as the creation and development of an economic and social system based upon Christian, social and economic principles, the achievement of the 'dignity and liberty of the individual' and the development of the country's natural resources 'to increase the wealth and well-being of the people'.[31] On the same weekend, at the Cork City Fianna Fáil convention, the Minister for Lands, Seán Moylan, accused Clann na Poblachta, Clann na Talmhan and the Labour Party of communistic tendencies with the 'Director of Finance of Clann na Poblachta [Peadar Cowan]' receiving particular attention as he had yet to withdraw communist statements made 'when he has concerned with creating an organization called The Vanguard'. If these statements were not withdrawn 'the public must expect from Clann na Poblachta a purge amongst its members'.[32]

The Fianna Fáil cabinet met immediately after the by-elections and Eamon de Valera announced that a general election would be held early in the new year in what was clearly an attempt to catch Clann na Poblachta before the party had an opportunity to consolidate its by-election successes.[33] The election would take place once 'certain work in which the government is at present engaged' was completed, de Valera explained. The certain work was the redrawing of the constituencies, which increased the number of TDs by nine to 147, the number of three-seat constituencies was increased from 15 to 22, and the number of four-seat and five-seat constituencies from eight to nine. The three seven-seat constituencies were abolished.[34] The general election was staged on Wednesday 4 February 1948 and Clann na Poblachta nominated 93 candidates, contesting all constituencies. However, the party was chronically disorganized and had just an average of six branches per constituency.[35] Despite its comprehensive sets of policies Clann na Poblachta's slogan for the election campaign was blunt: 'Put them out'.

Peadar Cowan began his 1948 general election campaign for the party in Fairview on 14 December 1947 by claiming that Fianna Fáil would never again be in power, the party was split from top to bottom 'and its former supporters were coming to the Clann in thousands'.[36] In Monaghan, Cowan promised that Clann na Poblachta would introduce legislation to limit TD's expenses 'to reasonable-vouched expenses incurred by them in performance of their public duties'.[37] On occasions, he departed from stated party policy, which provided Fianna Fáil with an opportunity to attack the party. In mid-December, at a rally at Fairview, he promised that all prisoners regardless of the offence would have their sentences reviewed by Clann na Poblachta. Political prisoners would be immediately released 'in order to create a spirit of goodwill'. Cowan promised a suite of reforms that he was later to revisit in his *Dungeons deep* publication of 1960. These included free legal aid, a complete overhaul of the Department of Justice, modernization of systems and methods of punishment and places of detention, a new approach to juvenile delinquency and to the 'training, education, and maintenance of neglected, abandoned and illegitimate children'. The proposals also included the establishment of an independent committee to review prison sentences and a guarantee to place judicial appointments 'outside the reach of political wire pullers'. 'Political pull is a poor and dangerous substitute for legal ability as a qualification for appointment to the bench'. The Minister for Finance, Frank Aiken, responded on this occasion and accused the 'would-be Minister' of wishing to release everyone who 'proves he tried to overthrow the democratic Republic established in 1937 by murdering or attacking members of the Forces who protected our people during the world war'. The gentlemen of Clann na Poblachta propose to make the state with the help of Cowan and 'the other splinter groups a lawyers' and lawbreakers' paradise'.[38] Speaking at Mountjoy Square in Dublin, Cowan explained elements of the party's agricultural policy. The party planned to make available the essential machinery required for maximum production at cost price to parish agricultural committees. The machinery would be owned cooperatively by the famers of the parish and the committees would be encouraged and helped to market produce and purchase seeds, fertilisers and other requirements on a cooperative basis. The National Agricultural Council would form a type of farmers' parliament that would deal with all agricultural matters and within limits prescribed by law would fix the price for all agricultural produce. The national council would be formed from regional agricultural councils democratically elected. Later in the week, Cowan delivered the same message at a party rally in Granard, Co. Longford.[39] The party's education policy provided the main theme for Cowan's address at Marino in Dublin. Free primary education for all children under 16 years of age was planned and this included books, requisites and a mid-day meal for all children. Free secondary and university education would also be available to talented students capable of passing the required entrance examinations complete with free maintenance, text books and travelling expenses. The party planned a radical change in the manner in which Irish was taught. It would be taught to all classes in primary schools in the manner favoured by the INTO but the policy of teaching all subjects to students who did not understand Irish through the medium would be abandoned as it was 'a cruel experiment on our children and was a tragic and colossal failure'.[40]

Cowan secured his seat in 1948 despite the best efforts of Fianna Fáil to damage his reputation and campaign. The Minister for Local Government, Seán MacEntee, was the character assassin in chief and the chief propagandist for Fianna Fáil's communist scare tactics. He engaged in the Don Quixote role of 'tilting gaily at Communist windmills, and smelling Bolsheviks behind every bush' according to an *Irish Times* editorial as it questioned why MacEntee devoted so much energy to 'this silly crusade against a non-existent threat to the national security' before concluding that 'Mr MacEntee seems to have Bolshevism on the brain'.[41] MacEntee focussed on three targets in particular: the Labour Party, Seán MacBride's previous association with Saor Éire, 'the red IRA', and Peadar Cowan. The attacks were partly designed to curb the propensity of opposition parties to transfer to each other, a trend that was first revealed in the presidential election of 1945.

A substantial file compiled by Peter Berry, head of the intelligence division in the Department of Justice, based on information supplied by the Special Branch on what were regarded as Cowan's communist activities, was made available to MacEntee. The information in Cowan's personal file included gems of subversion such as that he 'frequented the Communist Bookshop "New Books" in 1945, '46, '47'; he was seen in the company of 'O'Neill, Nolan, Fitzgerald [known communists] ... in Mooney's public house' and most damning of all 'he was present with Con Lehane and others at a lecture given by Seán Murray in Jury's Hotel, November 1943 on "From Czarism to Stalin" which ended with the singing of the Internationale'. Peter Berry wasn't the only one who kept MacEntee supplied with propaganda material. The Meath–Westmeath Fianna Fáil TD, M.J. Kennedy, wrote to MacEntee, on 19 July 1946, and informed him that

> There is a small monthly called Irish Review printed in Argus Office in Drogheda. I send you outer cover. It is 100% communistic. Copies should be filed by Information Bureau. I also send Cowan's letter to *Meath Chronicle*.

M.J. Costello also offered to supply MacEntee with information on a confidential basis on Cowan's army career that would discredit the Clann na Poblachta executive member.[42] One of those who came to Cowan's defence was M.J. Kennedy's party colleague in Meath, Jim Hilliard, who pointed out that he 'was the father of eleven children and a very good practising Catholic'.[43] In a Communism in Ireland file, his role as a Labour Party organizer was also included in this catalogue of alleged communist activities: he assisted James Larkin junior and John de Courcy Ireland in founding the Dublin executive of the Labour Party, which 'had a predominantly communist personnel'; he played a prominent part in the red executive of the Labour Party; he was a close associate of a certain Donal O'Reilly, a member of the Dublin co-ordinating committee of the Communist Party of Ireland; in 1944, he attempted to start the Vanguard movement which had 'as one of its aims the destruction of capitalism and the establishment of a socialist republic in Ireland' and in his speech to launch the new organization he claimed that 'socialism is the next development due in Ireland'.[44] It was also suggested that his 'attitude and conduct indicate that he is closely in touch with and probably tutored by the leading Communists here'.[45]

Cowan's inclusion in the MacEntee hit-list was partly inspired by fears in Fianna Fáil about the formation of a Labour–Clann na Poblachta alliance but there was more to it than that as the minister pointed out to Tommy Mullins (Fianna Fáil's general secretary) in July 1947: 'If the [Cowan] material were used properly it would probably do one of two things, either split Clann na Poblachta by driving Cowan and his followers out of it or else kill Clann na Poblachta in the rural areas'.[46] MacEntee launched his campaign of vilification at the Fianna Fáil convention to select candidates for the Dublin North-East constituency in mid-December when he stated that much more important issues than the price of beer or tobacco were at stake. Western democracies were threatened by the same forces that had overrun the Christian people of eastern Europe; 'the forces of Russian Communism had selected Ireland, in the company of the Vatican, Spain and Portugal for a special attack'. Trade unions had been infiltrated and turned into instruments of foreign conquest. 'Nationalism had been used as a camouflage for Communism'. Communists played a very large part in Irish political parties, MacEntee claimed. 'Mr Norton's Labour Party was undoubtedly one. Clann na Poblachta was an organization which had associated with it men and women communist in everything except their acceptance of the name'. Peadar Cowan was included in a list of those associated with organizations such as Saor Éire, launched by Seán MacBride in 1931 and condemned in a Bishops' pastoral as an organization that was 'frankly Communist in its aims'; 'Friends of Soviet Russia, the Irish Communist Party, the Republican Congress and The Vanguard' also posed threats to Irish democracy.[47] This basic message was repeated by MacEntee throughout the campaign and was diligently reported in the *Irish Press* which devoted 76 per cent of its column inches to the Fianna Fáil party compared to just 6 per cent for Clann na Poblachta and 18 per cent for the

4. Extract from Seán MacEntee's letter to *Irish Press* of 20 Jan. 1948 targeting Peadar Cowan

Mr. Cowan's claims to notoriety rest on another basis. He is, first of all, the man who, as Director of Organisation of the Labour Party in 1943, gave the pass to the Communists and allowed them to capture the Dublin Executive of the Party. In relation to this matter a leading Dublin Communist, in congratulating his fellow "Comrades" on the success of the infiltration policy which had been pursued by them, referred to the placing of two Communist members, James Larkin, junior, and John de Courcy Ireland, as Chairman and Secretary, respectively, of the Dublin Executive of the Labour Party, with virtual control of that body and the winning over to their side of the Director of Organisation, Captain Peadar Cowan.

Again to Mr. Cowan' belongs the honour of being founder of the "Vanguard." In the "Vanguard" Mr Cowan proposed, among other things:

(a) The destruction of capitalism the establishment of a Socialist (i.e., Communist) Republic here, and the assimilation of that Communist State, in a European Federation of Socialist (i.e., Communist) Republics.

(b) Public control of industries.

(c) That the distribution of esssential commodities be organised on co-operative lines under State control, i.e., shopkeepers, like "kulaks" were to be liquidated, as in Russia.

(d) All dwellinghouses not occupied by their owners to be acquired by the State. All houses for letting to be under the direct control of the State—just as in Russia, where, if a man is not a loyal and obedient tool of the Communist Party, he and his family may sleep in a shed.

Lastly, to Mr. Cowan belongs the fame of proclaiming, on September 29th, 1944, the ultimate world-triumph of Communism in these words:

"The world situation to-day is composed of four ideologies — Communism, Fascism, National Socialism and the Corporate State, and of these the last three will disappear."

It will be noted (a) that Mr. Cowan singled out Communism as being the worthiest to survive and (b) that democracy finds no place in his scheme of things.

other parties and independent candidates.[48] At the time, letters to the newspapers were the principal means by which political arguments were articulated and differences dissected. MacEntee and Cowan were prolific and formidable letter writers and a regular pattern developed as MacEntee's claims were rejected, repeated and rejected again with the letters page of the *Irish Press* the medium for the exchange of propaganda and counter-propaganda (fig. 4).

In mid-January, MacEntee claimed that Seán MacBride and Cowan had quarrelled and that MacBride was trying to oust him from the party before claiming that 'it will take more than Mr Cowan's expulsion to cleanse Clann na Poblachta of Communism'. This claim was rejected by Cowan as 'false, malicious, unscrupulous and reckless. Seán MacBride and I are personal friends and loyal colleagues and as joint founders and executive members of Clann na Poblachta, we are working loyally together to attain the aims and objectives of Clann na Poblachta'.[49] MacEntee countered that from a selfish political point of view he was glad to receive the assurance that MacBride was not 'endeavouring to jettison the founder of The Vanguard', and accepted the assurance 'with all due gratitude to Mr MacBride'. He then claimed that in 1933 Cowan was 'a leading member of the Fine Gael Blueshirts, who did not, however, meet with the approval of General Seán MacEoin, for reasons well known to Mr Cowan'. MacEntee documented how the manifesto of The Vanguard movement promoted communism by inserting his own explanations of the ideas in a manner that suggested they were part of the original manifesto. Where socialism was used in a letter, for example, communism was added in parenthesis, or as Cowan stated in his response published in the *Irish Press* 'most of the alleged [Vanguard] proposals are comment and insertions by Mr MacEntee himself'. Cowan emphatically rejected 'the defamatory statements and allegations', denied that he was ever a member of the Blueshirts and claimed that 'An eminent Doctor of Philosophy and former Professor of Maynooth' assured him that 'there is not one word in the Manifesto of The Vanguard contrary to Catholic philosophy, Catholic teaching', an assurance that helped him 'to bear a bitter campaign of slander over a period of years without complaint'.[50] He was again forced to deny MacEntee's claims and in a short letter to the *Irish Press* on 29 January 1948 wrote 'I am not and never have been a member of the Communist Party of Ireland and am not a communist'.[51]

PEADAR COWAN AND THE INTER-PARTY GOVERNMENT

The election results confirmed MacEntee's worst fears and the Dáil arithmetic facilitated the removal of Fianna Fáil from office for the first time since 1932. Fianna Fáil lost eight seats and returned only 68 TDs, despite the extra seats available. The early election checked the Clann na Poblachta advance and the party won just 10 seats, far less than expected. Fine Gael won 31 seats, the Labour Party 14, and five National Labour Party members were elected as well as seven Clann na Talmhan TDs and 12 independents.[52] Peadar Cowan at the fifth attempt was finally elected for the Dublin North-East constituency polling 4,692 first preference votes in a constituency where Clann na Poblachta attracted 15.5 per cent of the first preference votes.[53] The arithmetic facilitated the removal of Fianna Fáil from power for the first time in sixteen years. An inter-party government, 'a patchwork of all organized non-Fianna Fáil parliamentary opinion', was formed comprising Fine Gael, Labour, National Labour, Clann na Talmhan and Clann na Poblachta and took office on 18 February 1948 when John A. Costello was elected Taoiseach by 75 votes to 68.[54]

One of the most ideologically diverse governments in the history of the state was formed, united by their unanimous wish to see Eamon de Valera and his party removed from power and their own desire to hold on to power for as long as possible. The government soon became faction-ridden and, as Dermot Keogh explains, the ideological diversity of cabinet members was accentuated by the swift manifestation of personal animosities within, and between, parties.[55] The marriage of political minds between Seán MacBride and Peadar Cowan was not to survive, and the relationship began to unravel almost as soon as the election results were announced. Their initial disagreements centred on the decision to enter government and the nomination of Noël Browne as Minister for Health. Cowan believed that Browne was too young and inexperienced for a key ministerial portfolio and that the party's involvement in government would serve to silence members from criticizing or questioning policy. He was also concerned about the potential loss of identity for the party as part of a multi-party government. The party executive members including Cowan unanimously agreed to vote Fianna Fáil out of office but Cowan and others opposed the party's acceptance of ministerial office but this proposal was defeated by eighteen votes to twelve. He later claimed that his motion not to take ministerial office seemed likely to be passed until Seán MacBride threatened to have those who opposed him expelled from the party. 'A few members changed sides and after this speech my motion was narrowly defeated'. He also claimed that MacBride should have given the parliamentary party the opportunity to discuss the issue and had he done so he believed that a different decision would have been made and Con Lehane would have been nominated to a ministerial post with MacBride and different ministries would have been chosen.[56] Cowan later claimed when the decision was taken it was made perfectly clear that members of Clann na Poblachta were free to criticize the government on all matters that conflicted with party policy.[57] Eithne MacDermott, who had sight of Cowan's unpublished memoirs, has written that prior to the meeting he met with MacBride to discuss the formation of the government. MacBride wished to obtain Cowan's agreement in advance of the party's national executive meeting and explained that he intended to accept the External Affairs ministerial portfolio as it would give him more time to build up Clann na Poblachta.[58]

PEADAR COWAN AND CLANN NA POBLACHTA: THE PARTING OF THE WAYS

Within five months of the formation of the inter-party government, Cowan was expelled from Clann na Poblachta. In the Dáil, he spoke against the Paris Convention and the agreement between the US and Ireland on the Marshall Aid proposals. MacBride believed that Cowan was not giving Clann na Poblachta the loyalty that was expected and his proposal to have him expelled from the party with a request that he resign his Dáil seat was carried by 35 votes to five on 3 July 1948.[59] Earlier in the new Dáil, Seán MacBride was 'personally embarrassed' by a request from Cowan to the Taoiseach, John A. Costello, to issue a statement on the Paris Convention. Arising from that matter, a party decision was taken that no questions that embarrassed a ministerial member of the party would be raised in the Dáil. Later, Cowan, supported by two party colleagues, at the committee stage proposed amendments to a Local Elections Bill to have the elections held in 1949 rather than in 1950. The amendment was rejected by the Minister for Local Government, Tim Murphy. Seán Lemass called a division, Cowan voted against the government and in favour of his own amendment. As no party discussion on the matter had taken place prior to the vote, Cowan's claim that he was supporting party policy enabled him to escape with a 'mild censure'.[60]

On 1 July, the Dáil debated the Convention for European Economic Co-operation, which was signed and accepted by sixteen European nations at Paris on 16 April 1948 and the bilateral Economic Co-operation Agreement between Ireland and the United States, the agreement which provided Marshall Aid to the country. Seán MacBride was the minister most directly involved in negotiating the agreement as the Marshall Aid brief fell within the Department of External Affairs. He travelled to Washington in May 1948 and negotiated a Marshall Aid package of £36 million, 87 per cent of which was in loan form, substantially short of the £120 million grant aid with which he hoped to secure to transform the country.[61] As the minister responsible, MacBride led the Dáil debate. The lengthiest contribution opposing the agreements came from Peadar Cowan who argued that the agreement required the 'surrender of certain of our national rights' without apparent reason or justification: 'We are not a beggar nation nor are we a mendicant nation'. He argued that Marshall Aid was designed to promote the foreign policy of the United States and it had as its objective the maintenance, strength and stability of the United States. Clann na Poblachta stressed in its election policy the necessity for absolute control of our own monetary system and currency. An agreement was now made with the United States of America 'to stabilize our currency, establish or maintain a valid rate of exchange, and balance our budget'; for Cowan this was 'an insulting agreement into which to enter with any other country'. The agreement also required a commitment to reduce public and private barriers to trade between the countries of western Europe, a commitment that required 'the surrender of our sovereignty in certain respects and certainly the surrender of our rights'. The one-sided agreement was the equivalent of 'buying a pig in a poke' and gave 'rights to America that America should not have in this country'.

As far as MacBride was concerned much of the criticism was 'based upon a complete misconception or misinterpretation of the terms of the agreement'.[62] The agreement received Dáil approval without a division. Two days later, on 3 July 1948, the Clann na Poblachta National Executive voted to expel Cowan for 'disloyalty to the organization' according to the official statement. Cowan's claim that a party meeting of 29 June had not made a formal decision on the agreement because MacBride, Nöel Browne and Con Lehane were absent made no impression on the party executive members on this occasion.[63] Instead, the standing committee of Clann na Poblachta pointed out that MacBride had made a statement about the convention in March and that Cowan at no point indicated any objection to the Marshall Plan in general.[64]

Despite his expulsion, Cowan committed to continue to 'press for the achievement of the aims, objectives and ideals' of Clann na Poblachta in accordance with the policy and programme of the party and pledges made to his constituents during the election campaign. However, he refused to commit to continue to support the government. He was expelled, he claimed, because he resisted attempts to make him a 'Yes man'.[65]

4. The independent Dáil deputy

Peadar Cowan spent just five months of his time in Dáil Éireann as a member of Clann na Poblachta. In this chapter some of his most significant parliamentary contributions, as an independent deputy, will be examined. Apart from the events surrounding the mother and child crisis, the most controversial episode in the history of the inter-party government was the declaration of a republic in 1949 and the repeal of the External Relations Act (1936). Taoiseach John A. Costello made the surprise announcement of the government's intention to repeal the External Relations Act at a press conference in Ottawa in Canada when he confirmed a *Sunday Independent* story of 5 September 1948. At the press conference, Costello stated that the act was full of inaccuracies and infirmities and the only remedy for it was to scrap it. He confirmed that Ireland was to leave the British Commonwealth and added that he saw no reason why Ireland could not continue in association with Britain but not as a member of the Commonwealth.[1] Historians disagree on the circumstances that inspired the surprise decision but Peadar Cowan is credited with having played a role with his questions from the back benches of Dáil Éireann unnerving the government. After his expulsion from Clann na Poblachta, Cowan attempted on a number of occasions to extract from John A. Costello a precise definition of Ireland's status and relationship with the Commonwealth beginning on 28 July when he asked 'when and in what circumstances Ireland ceased to be a member of the British Commonwealth of Nations?' Costello explained that Ireland was a sovereign independent democratic state as defined in Article 5 of the Constitution, and was associated with the members of the British Commonwealth. 'The process by which Ireland ceased formally to be a member of that Commonwealth has been one of gradual development'.[2] Cowan wasn't satisfied and returned to the issue on 5 August with a query to Costello on the circumstances and the authority by which Ireland became associated with the Commonwealth and the obligations associated with this arrangement. He also asked whether Ireland was an independent republic and if not 'whether he will indicate what constitutional, statutory or other steps are necessary to declare and establish Ireland as an independent republic'. In his response, Costello claimed that 'no useful purpose would be served' by explaining the circumstances by which Ireland became associated with the members of the Commonwealth, 'the Commonwealth is a free association, which, by virtue of its very freedom, could be determined by unilateral action'. The question of whether Ireland is a republic was 'purely one of nomenclature', which he was not prepared to discuss. Ireland, by its Constitution, was a sovereign, independent, democratic state.[3] Cowan at this stage was the one most likely to introduce a private member's bill to repeal the External Relations Act, a move that would be politically devastating for the inter-party government and of course provide more embarrassment for his arch political enemy, the Minister for External Affairs, Seán MacBride. This anxiety may have helped trigger Costello's surprise announcement in Canada and the Republic of Ireland Act came into effect on Easter Monday 1949.

'ACTION NOT TALK WILL END PARTITION'

In early 1950, Cowan engaged in what can only be described as an act of dangerous political madness. The man who believed that the main lesson to be taken from the events prior to the Civil War was the importance of having the army under civilian control now set about establishing a military force to invade Northern Ireland and reclaim the territory under British jurisdiction. An ambivalence existed towards the use of violence at the time as a means of achieving Irish unity and this was reflected at the Clann na Poblachta Ard Fheis held on 5 June 1949.[4] A motion that force should be used if necessary to reunite the country received strong support but was eventually defeated after a long debate.[5] As David McCullagh has suggested, Peadar Cowan attempted to tap into this ambivalence when he embarked on his recruitment crusade and this is the most generous interpretation that can be given to this escapade. It also drew attention to the total failure of the all-party, anti-partitionist Mansion House committee, which proved to be nothing more than a propaganda machine churning out anti-unionist bombast.[6] On 4 February 1950 some of the national newspapers reported on an advertisement carried by the *Irish Press* from Cowan headed 'Partition Must be Ended' that rejected constitutional methods as a means of ending partition. 'They have talked and talked about Partition, for nearly thirty years and they are still talking about it. But all their talk has been futile and useless.' 'Talk has never achieved anything and will never achieve anything. Action not talk will end Partition ...' the advertisement read.[7] The new organization made its first public appearance on 15 May 1950, when about 50 men headed by Cowan marched through Dublin in military formation and responded to military commands. An estimated 800 people attended the public meeting that followed where Cowan promised that 'the force will be so organized that it will move across the border and take possession of the Six Counties within a day'. There was no intention of engaging in isolated incidents such 'as taking over a particular barracks, or house, or blowing up a bridge'. He claimed that the movement included men who had fought in 1916, 1921 and 1922; others had fought in the recent war in North Africa, and others had landed in France on D-Day. 'A grand fifth-column' was being organized in Northern Ireland.[8]

When it was not subjecting the initiative to 'chocolate soldiery' ridicule, the *Irish Times* explored the dangers inherent in 'the down-to-bedrock foolhardiness of Captain Peadar Cowan' and his plan.[9] In an editorial of 20 May 1950, the potential of Cowan's 'dark counsel' to influence young Irishmen who have been 'hearing nothing but violent abuse of their fellow countrymen in the North during the last couple of years' was noted. It was therefore no surprise that sooner or later 'somebody like Captain Cowan should come along with the threat of armed action in an effort to take advantage of the hot blood that always is to be found amongst young Irishmen'. The foolishness of the scheme was underlined when it was realized that the Irish Army was dependent on the British Army for military supplies for training purposes. 'Has he the remotest idea of the realities of his proposed invasion, or is he aware of the immeasurable harm that his wild words are calculated to do to the cause of Irish unity?' Cowan's reference to the organization of 'a grand fifth-column' in Northern Ireland was particularly dangerous. 'Could a more irresponsible utterance be imagined' the editorial asked; it 'provided a direct incitement to the Northern extremists to harden their hearts against the Nationalists'. The 'scatter-brained' invasion project was 'presumably designed to attract international attention on Ireland's grievance – that the time had come for another Easter Week – but, surely the nation has had more than enough of blood-baths'.[10] Cowan continued to campaign and at Doyle's Corner in Phibsborough, the message that partition could only be ended by violence was repeated along with the claim that it was in Britain's interest to keep the country divided. Britain was in a perilous state and 'with the British Empire weak, that was the time to hit it'. Government failure to make a real effort to end partition was 'a disgrace to the memory of the men who had given their all for Ireland in the years between 1916 and 1921'.[11]

Eamon de Valera raised the matter of Cowan's private volunteer army and posed a question to Taoiseach John A. Costello on the government's attitude to Cowan's actions and on what steps the government was taking to vindicate Article 15 (6) of the Constitution, which vested the right to maintain armed forces exclusively to the Oireachtas. De Valera was assured that the 'provisions of the Article of the Constitution referred to have been and will continue to be vindicated by the government' and that 'Nothing that has occurred or is occurring is in any way as serious as the Deputy suggests'.[12] The matter was also raised in the Dáil during the debate on the Justice estimates when Gerald Boland called on the Minister for Justice, Seán MacEoin, to ban Cowan's volunteers on the basis that although Cowan was 'more or less play-acting, some of the people he may induce to take part in this volunteer organization may not be play-acting'. Others might be more serious and the government should not wait until shooting started. Cowan might be 'a sawdust Caesar' but the minister was not entitled to be complacent. 'Small things like this lead to very serious results'.[13]

Michael Moran (Fianna Fáil) also addressed the issue pointing out that it was the duty of the minister 'to see that those people, even amongst themselves, must be prevented from shooting themselves'. It should be made clear to the people that there is only one army in the country and it is under the control of the state. Seán MacEntee also engaged in the debate. The volunteer force was 'full of danger, internal and external, to the peace of this country' and he called for the use of the Offences Against the State Act against Cowan. The debate provided Seán MacEntee with another opportunity to forensically discredit Cowan's political career as he endeavoured to prove that the force was being 'organised to serve other ends'. Cowan's time as the Director of Organization of the Labour Party and its alleged association with the Communist Party was referenced as was his association with the Vanguard movement established to 'destroy capitalism and establish socialism in Ireland'. In his response, the Minister for Justice, General Seán MacEoin, replied that he was dealing with Cowan in the same way as the previous government by doing nothing 'and by ignoring the whole situation'. He had nothing more to add to John A. Costello's assurance given to Eamon de Valera that 'the Constitution would be maintained and upheld'. He added that the only people who had assisted Cowan in the establishment of his 'so called force' were the members of Fianna Fáil by attracting attention to the recruitment campaign. The *Irish Press* was the only paper in the state to advertise the 'private army as such'.[14]

The *Irish Times* correctly predicted that Cowan's 'war-like preparations' was the 'sort of stuff that Six-County propagandists' dreams are made on'. In a Stormont debate in November 1950 it was revealed that a reserve of B Specials had been established at Ballykinlar Military Camp, Co. Down, 'in consequence of threats made by a gentleman in the South, who had threatened to come and cut the throat of all loyalists'. Later in the month, the existence of Cowan's volunteers was used to justify the approval of £45,000 for the B Special force. In the Northern Ireland Senate debate, the Deputy Speaker, Herbert Quinn, stated that as long as threats such as those made by Captain Cowan existed, his desire was to see the 'Constabulary forces in Northern Ireland increased and maintained'.[15] The unfiltered madness of the scheme had on this occasion achieved a result diametrically opposite to Cowan's intention: partition had been solidified.

THE MOTHER AND CHILD SCHEME

Noël Browne, the Minister for Health, was conspicuously successful in tackling the scourge of TB in the first two years of his ministry. At the same time, as Cowan was engaging in his extra-parliamentary activity, Browne was engaged in a far more significant struggle with the bishops, and the doctors of the Irish Medical Association (IMA) and ultimately with his fellow cabinet members as he pressed ahead with his scheme to implement what has become known as the mother and child scheme. The scheme proposed to provide all mothers and children under 16 years of age with free medical care.[16] Episcopal opposition led by Archbishop John Charles McQuaid of Dublin and Dr Michael Browne of Galway combined with objections from the medical profession frustrated the minister's intentions. The IMA condemned the plan and in a ballot of its members the proposed scheme was rejected by a margin of 80 per cent.[17] The hierarchy's opposition to the proposed scheme was outlined to the Taoiseach, John A. Costello, on 10 October 1950. The intended scheme 'was in direct opposition to the rights of the family and the individual and was liable to very great abuse'. The bishops' correspondence specified that the 'right to provide for the health of children belongs to parents, not to the state ... If adopted in law they would constitute a ready-made instrument for future totalitarian aggression.' The state's right to intervene was limited to the necessitous or negligent families who comprised no more than 10 per cent of all family groups. The bishops regarded with 'the greatest apprehension' the proposal to give local medical officers the right to provide Irish women and girls education in regard to motherhood including 'instruction in sex relations, chastity and marriage', a sphere of conduct at 'once so delicate and sacred'. There was no guarantee that gynaecological care delivered by state officials, especially those 'trained in institutions in which we have no confidence', would respect 'Catholic principles'. After exchanges of correspondence and intermittent meetings with the bishops, Dr Browne apparently believed that he had dealt with the concerns of the hierarchy and on 6 March 1951 published details of the scheme. An explanatory brochure was sent to all members of the hierarchy. The scheme proposed to provide children under 16 years of age with free medical care including inoculations and injections, at school and at home, and for all illnesses, free specialist, consultant, surgical and hospital treatment as well as free dental and eye care. A choice of doctor was available including the family doctor provided he or she engaged with the scheme. There was no compulsion, no means test and no contributions were required.[18] Dr John Charles McQuaid responded by letter to both Noël Browne and John A. Costello on 8 March reiterating 'each and every objection' made by the bishops when they originally met with Dr Browne in October. John A. Costello advised Noël Browne to engage with the bishops 'so as to remove any grounds for objection on their part' and to 'find a mutually beneficial satisfactory solution of the difficulties which have arisen'. No solution was found and at a cabinet meeting on 6 April each of Noël Browne's ministerial colleagues refused to support the scheme. Dr Browne left the meeting and asked for time to consider his position. In his absence, it was quickly agreed to abandon the scheme and replace it with a less controversial one that included a means test and was 'in conformity with Catholic social teaching'. On 10 April, Seán MacBride wrote to Dr Browne and requested him to tender his resignation to the Taoiseach. The following day the minister complied with the request.[19]

The controversy and the resignation of Dr Noël Browne instigated the most extended debate on church-state relations in the country that had taken place to that point in time.[20] The minister himself provided much of the information for the discussion when on the evening of his resignation, he released to the *Irish Times* the correspondence exchanged between himself, the bishops and John A. Costello.[21] The great power of the hierarchy in Ireland was exposed to public scrutiny and the correspondence 'documented the secret ways in which the clerics routinely bypassed democratic channels in influencing government policy'.[22] The *Irish Times* initiated the debate with an editorial that proclaimed 'This is a sad day for Ireland. … an honest, far-sighted and energetic man has been driven out of active politics. The most serious revelation, however, is that the Roman Catholic Church would seem to be the effective government of this country'.[23] The Dáil debate provided evidence to support this claim as ministers and deputies proclaimed their acceptance of the Catholic church's authority on the matter. 'I, as a Catholic obey my Church authorities and will continue to do so, in spite of the *Irish Times* or anything else', Taoiseach John A. Costello told his fellow parliamentarians. His ministerial colleagues concurred. Seán MacBride agreed. 'Those of us in this House who are Catholics, and all of us in the government who are Catholics are, as such of course, bound to give obedience to the rulings of our Church and of our hierarchy'. Even Noël Browne, in his resignation speech, accepted the primacy of the bishops: 'Even I as a Catholic accept unequivocally, and unreservedly the views of the hierarchy on the matter'.[24]

A moment of truth had arrived for Peadar Cowan. Eithne MacDermott has pointed out that following Peadar Cowan's expulsion from Clann na Poblachta 'what had commenced as a policy disagreement turned into a form of mutual personal detestation, as he and MacBride were to spend a considerable amount of time over the next few years exchanging a substantial volume of personal abuse in the Dáil' as Cowan employed what the *Irish Times* described as 'commando tactics against the former guerrilla leader'.[25] Noël Browne's resignation provided a perfect opportunity for Cowan to express his detestation of his erstwhile leader. He was unconditional in his support of Browne who was implementing what was Clann na Poblachta policy. He was the only TD to explore the secret manipulative machinations of the hierarchy and the legitimacy of this interference in the affairs of the state. Peadar Cowan initially focused on MacBride's entitlement to seek the resignation of a minister and pointed out 'that this action by Mr MacBride was unlawful and unconstitutional and a breach of the privileges of the Dáil'. This was technically correct but John A. Costello had allowed MacBride to request Browne's resignation out of courtesy to his role as party leader, and if MacBride had not done so or if he refused to step down, Costello was prepared to intervene.[26] Cowan accused MacBride of destroying the career of a man who 'has built a monument to himself in the health services of this country in a short period of three years.'

This is an unfortunate and most tragic affair. It is unfortunate that within this inter-party Government which, in my opinion, has been doing magnificent work, a crisis of this kind should have arisen. It is regrettable that personalities should have entered into the matter in the way they have ... It struck me as a thunderbolt on Friday last to learn that a situation had arisen in which one of the most popular ministers in the government was on the verge of being dismissed or resigning ... When I heard the opening remarks in regard to him, by a person who was his Leader [MacBride], as he likes to call himself, who was his colleague; when I see the bitterness that is in that man against Deputy Dr Noël Browne, I feel ashamed of our democratic institutions. Why has Deputy Dr Browne, from being the minister that was held up by Clann na Poblachta all over the country as such a wonderful man, been brought to the position that he is described as a scoundrel and a liar, as incompetent, incapable and unfit to be minister in this or any other government? What has brought about that change? Is it not clear that what has brought about the change is that Deputy Dr Browne, because of his great work for the people, was becoming more popular than his leader.[27]

Cowan claimed that attempts to rescue the situation 'were deliberately sabotaged by the Minister for External Affairs [MacBride] who wanted Dr Browne's scalp at all costs. I feel compelled to say these things and to make no bones about the fact that I consider the Minister for External Affairs to be one of the most dangerous characters in this country'.[28] When the Dáil debate resumed on 17 April, Peadar Cowan continued to claim that personal animosity and jealousy were responsible for the minister's downfall. It was clear, 'that the Minister for External Affairs was violently opposed to Deputy Dr Browne for personal reasons. In the executive of Clann na Poblachta, Deputy Dr Browne stood for honesty and the Minister for External Affairs stood for compromise, for surrender and for expediency'. He had 'engaged in a conspiracy to destroy his party colleague and fellow minister'.[29]

In his contribution to the debate, Cowan also made it absolutely clear that the bishops had no authority whatsoever to interfere privately in the business of the Dáil. The bishops had stepped outside their legitimate sphere: 'the most disquieting feature of this sorry business' was 'the revelation that the real government of the country may not, in fact, be exercised by the elected representatives of the people as we believed it was but by the Bishops, meeting secretly and enforcing their rule by means of private interviews with ministers and by documents of a secret and confidential nature sent by them to ministers and to the head of the alleged government of the state'. As a Catholic (in the words of Noël Browne, he was what is known in Ireland 'as a deeply religious man'),[30] Cowan objected to the 'usurpation of the authority of the government by the bishops', and as a Catholic he protested against 'this secretive, occult and objectionable practice'. As a member of Dáil Éireann, and as a representative of the people he was entitled to be fully informed of all the factors involved in the consideration of legislation. Therefore, he informed Dáil Éireann that

> It is wrong, morally wrong, for the bishops to keep them and me in the dark and to exercise control in civil affairs behind their and my back in regard to matters to which they as citizens and I as their representative have express authority under the constitution of this country to deal with. That control was exercised by the bishops over the government, and that control was accepted and tolerated by the government without the knowledge of Dáil Éireann or of the people, and the public has been shocked by the revelation that that has been the position.[31]

The more general issue of the legitimacy of episcopal influence was also examined by Cowan in his contribution and he concluded that on this occasion the bishops had stepped outside their legitimate domain. He distinguished between public and private representation: 'The Catholic hierarchy are entitled to express their views on all matters of public welfare, as are the clergy of all denominations'. Their views are entitled to respect and consideration but they must be expressed in public and made known to every citizen. The parliament that fails to insist on this is failing in its duty. 'If we do not, our democracy is a fraud, our Constitution a sham, and our general elections humbug, pretence and swindle'.[32] He asserted that 'there is no conflict with Catholic social teaching in the provision of a free for all mother and child scheme … if the government accept the dictation of the bishops in this matter, then they are flaunting the Constitution of this country and they are acting contrary to their duty as representatives of the people'. The bishops had stepped outside their legitimate sphere and in doing so they 'trespass on the domain and seek to usurp the powers of the legitimate civil authority. In so doing they act contrary to the provisions of the Constitution of this country'.

> The Bishops deal with State taxation, which is a matter for this House and this House alone. They give views on facts, express prophetic opinions and seek to determine the meaning of, or the inferences to be drawn from matters, as any student of moral theology knows, that are not within the definition of Catholic doctrine on which the Bishops may speak with authority to Catholics.[33]

In the ensuing fallout, Noël Browne and Jack McQuillan resigned from Clann na Poblachta and joined Peadar Cowan on the backbenches. The inter-party government collapsed within a month and the Dáil was dissolved on 5 May after the government was threatened with defeat on the price of milk. In the general election, the Clann na Poblachta party was routed, securing only two seats. The party's vote declined from 274,000 to 54,260; just 26 candidates faced the electorate compared to 93 in 1948.[34] The party topped the league table of those who lost their deposits with fourteen candidates losing out. Peadar Cowan, Noël Browne and Jack McQuillan were re-elected as independent deputies. Cowan polled 3,606 first preference votes in the Dublin North-East constituency in which Fianna Fáil's Oscar Traynor (13,192) and independent Alfie Byrne (10,397) comfortably exceeded the quota of 7,827 on the first count. Cowan received 131 of Traynor's transferred surplus and a crucial 566 from those of Alfie Byrne. He was eventually elected on the tenth count after receiving 823 votes when the final Fianna Fáil candidate was eliminated. Cowan's 5,795 votes placed him just 91 votes ahead of Labour's Denis Larkin, the last remaining candidate.[35] His re-election was considered by the *Irish Times* to have been 'one of the remarkable events of the election' as he held no public meetings and did little canvassing. However, Cowan made extensive use of what the *Longford Leader* called 'the vote entreaty van'. He engaged two such vans, one on his own behalf and 'the other lauding the praises of his wife', 'who was also a candidate for municipal honours'.[36] The *Irish Times* also ominously predicted that Cowan's return to the Dáil may have sealed the fate of the government.[37]

FROM 'A VANGUARD OF THE PEOPLE TO BEING A MUDGUARD OF FIANNA FÁIL'

The outcome of the election was effectively a hung Dáil and as politics is in large part the art of the possible, Peadar Cowan and Noël Browne swallowed hard on their principles and supported Eamon de Valera in the vote for Taoiseach and returned Fianna Fáil to power, an action that later inspired William Norton to remind Peadar Cowan that he had 'demoted himself from being a vanguard of the people to being a mudguard of Fianna Fáil'. When the 14th Dáil assembled to elect a new Taoiseach, the nomination of the outgoing Taoiseach John A. Costello was defeated by 74 votes to 72 and in the division that followed Eamon de Valera was elected Taoiseach by 74 votes to 69, with five independent deputies supporting the Fianna Fáil leader – with Jack McQuillan, one of three members abstaining.[38]

One of the great consistencies in Peadar Cowan's political career had been an unadulterated opposition to Fianna Fáil and Eamon de Valera and the articulation of his belief that the party and its leader represented a danger to democracy. On this occasion, Cowan's vote was one of the crucial votes responsible for returning de Valera to power. According to the record of the Dáil, Peadar Cowan met with John A. Costello prior to the vote and informed him that he was supporting Eamon de Valera in the vote for Taoiseach. Oliver J. Flanagan, who witnessed the conversation, informed the deputies that Cowan made it clear to Costello that he intended to vote for Fianna Fáil as a protest against the bishops dictating to the inter-party government.[39] Pragmatism is an occupational hazard of the politician but this decision by Cowan stretched the concept to well beyond breaking point, a decision he justified on the need to ensure stable government for the country. 'If I interpret correctly the mind of the people, they want a period of stable government ... I think that the [Fianna Fáil] bloc of 69, generally supported by a number of Independents, will give us a stable government', he informed the Dáil. He drew a distinction between Cowan, the individual and Cowan, the Dáil Deputy. As a deputy, it was necessary to vote for de Valera 'to ensure, so far as I can, stable government for the country'. Other justifications were also referenced: the actions of the inter-party government in 'throwing overboard', without the authority of the Dáil, the free-for-all mother and child scheme and replacing it with a scheme that included a means test; 'the unconstitutional action of the Minister for External Affairs in bringing about the resignation of the Minister for Health, Dr Browne, from the government'. Ignoring the impact his own recruiting activities had on the Unionist population, he focussed on the 'real fear' of 'our fellow countrymen in the six counties' that if 'they unite with us they will be ruled not by the lawful government but by the bishops'. Cowan claimed that the 'declarations and actions by the Taoiseach, the Tánaiste, the Minister for External Affairs and other ministers in connection with the mother and child scheme ... have unfortunately accentuated the fears and postponed the peaceful ending of partition'. 'Grave national damage' was done and if John A. Costello and his ministers were returned to office 'the prospect of a friendly settlement of the partition question would be seriously jeopardised'. As a believer in the 'ideals of James Connolly' he wished to provide the Labour Party with an opportunity to build a strong party 'based on the teachings and actuated by the principles of Connolly'. He had seen 'the Labour Party time after time weakened and defeated by its association with the forces of reaction'.[40] This arrogant lecturing to the Labour Party drew a response from Michael J. Keyes, Minister for Local Government in the outgoing administration. Keyes questioned his contribution to the Labour Party in the past: 'He has never contributed anything to the Labour philosophy of this country and he has no right to mention the late James Connolly or the Labour Party which was founded by him'. Keyes had no doubt that the real reason for his support for Fianna Fáil lay in his antipathy towards Seán MacBride and Clann na Poblachta: 'he has had his knife in the Minister for External Affairs, Deputy MacBride, who is the Leader of that Party'.[41] On this occasion, as Deputy Seán Collins was later to claim, Peadar Cowan had 'been able to succeed in political gymnastics that do not involve merely a one and a half somersault but a kind of concentrated gymnastic effort by which he can do one and a half somersaults forward and at the same time two somersaults backwards'.[42]

COWAN INSPIRED CONTROVERSY AT THE COUNCIL OF EUROPE

In 1953, Peadar Cowan was selected as a substitute member of the Irish delegation to the fifth consultative assembly of the Council of Europe at Strasbourg despite the reservations of several TDs.[43] William Norton did not travel to Strasburg and was replaced by Cowan. The appointment provided him with an opportunity to introduce his socialist sympathies to a wider European audience. In the opening session, Cowan struck a discordant note to the general denouncement of communism and warned that the US presented as great a threat to Europe's interests as Russia for which he was rebuked by James Crosbie, for what the leader of the delegation termed 'wholly irresponsible and grotesquely untrue statements'. When the conference reassembled in September, the context of European politics had greatly changed following the death of Stalin. The deep freeze associated with the Cold War was less chilling. The Irish delegation attacked communism and spoke of the need to reintegrate Germany fully into Europe. Cowan once again introduced a discordant note. He attacked a report on the international situation as being 'partial and biased' and warned that the general condemnation of Russia was unsustainable before turning his attention to Germany. 'Germany wants unification. She wanted it after the 1919 war; she wanted back her lost provinces. She wanted her place in the sun. She wants rearmament; she wanted it after the 1919 war. I see no change.' James Crosbie again rejected in 'the strongest terms the views expressed' by Cowan. 'All Irishmen', he explained, 'will regret that this occasion was used to make a speech calculated to reopen old wounds when all our efforts are directed towards the united effort of common action'.

Cowan's contribution provoked some debate in Ireland with the *Irish Times* a notable exception to the general press denouncement. Its editorial, entitled Captain Courageous, offered some qualified support to Cowan, which in turn encouraged Conor Cruise O'Brien to assure a German diplomat that the paper's views were unrepresentative of the Irish public before dismissing it as a paper that contained 'a blend of archaic Anglophilism with faintly leftism tendencies'. In the Dáil, Frank Aiken pointed out that delegates spoke in a personal capacity; the *Leader*, a Dublin periodical, was less generous and dismissive of Cowan: 'the tomfoolery, the pomposity and general clumsiness which so often characterizes our performances on the international stage' was unnecessary.[44]

Again Peadar Cowan put pen to paper to defend his contribution and responded to what he referred to as the 'violent personal attack' of the *Sunday Independent*. The newspaper was critical of his contribution at the assembly and of his inclusion in the delegation, an inclusion based on his support for Fianna Fáil according to the feature headed 'Cowan insults Germany'. The speech was 'a gratuitous insult to a people with whom this country is on the friendliest terms and with whom we are endeavouring to develop a valuable trade'. Cowan's behaviour was also likely to place the Irish people 'in a false position abroad. Foreigners cannot be expected to know that he speaks for nobody but himself'.[45] In his response, Cowan explained that he warned of the dangers of a revival of German militarism and reminded the delegates of the horrors of Belsen and other German camps and asked them 'not to forget that in the short period of less than seventy years German militarists brought about three great wars and caused the loss of millions of lives'. He also explained that those who attend a Council of Europe meeting do so as 'individuals and each speaks for himself', a freedom of discussion that is one of the council's great assets. The repudiation of his views by James Crosbie, one who was never elected to Dáil Éireann and 'failed even to secure election to the Senate', was for 'Fine Gael party purposes in Ireland'.[46] This fourth appearance of an Irish delegation at a Council of Europe assembly was part of a learning experience on the ways of international diplomacy; in the opinion of Michael Kennedy and Eunan O'Halpin, the performance of Irish politicians at council meetings and other fora 'seems never to have reached the depths witnessed in Strasbourg in 1953'.[47]

ASSAULT IN ARTANE

During the 1950s stories of abuse in industrial schools were known to certain politicians, civil servants and religious orders but were rarely acknowledged in the public domain. Peadar Cowan was the exception and on 23 April 1954, on his final day as a TD, he raised the issue following representations from a constituent whose son, an inmate of Artane Industrial School, was hospitalized following a vicious assault by a Christian Brother. Although Cowan tempered his account somewhat by classifying the episode of violence as an 'isolated incident' the account he presented to the Minister for Education, Seán Moylan, was truly shocking. The boy was punished following an incident with another pupil and was given a number of slaps on the hand with a leather strap. He refused to accept further punishment with the edge of the strap and grabbed a sweeping brush to defend himself. A second Christian Brother was sent for and 'seeing the brush in the boy's hands, snatched it from him, struck him on the head injuring him, struck him on the back injuring him, struck him on the arm and broke his arm', Cowan explained in the Dáil. The boy was taken to hospital and his arm set in plaster two days after the incident took place. The boy's mother was not informed of the injury and was initially refused a meeting with the Superior of Artane and was only allowed to see her son after Cowan's intervention, eight days after the incident took place. After learning of the incident, Cowan immediately contacted Seán Moylan and asked him to investigate the incident and informed him that he intended to raise the matter in the adjournment debate. In his Dáil contribution, Cowan sought a guarantee from the minister 'that an incident such as has occurred in this case will not be permitted to occur again' and an assurance 'that punishment, if it is to be inflicted on those sent to industrial schools, will be inflicted by some person of experience and responsibility. If punishment were to be imposed in a fit of hot temper, it would be exceptionally bad and, in fact, as in this case, it would be dangerous'. The incident 'profoundly shocked' Cowan and illustrated the necessity for the minister and the Department of Education to 'have the closest supervision of schools such as this, where children, many of them without parents at all, are sent to be brought up'.[48]

In the words of Aideen Carroll, Seán Moylan's biographer, the incident is 'one shadow that hangs over Moylan's tenure as Minister for Education'.[49] Moylan's views were rooted in the convictions of the time and his interest was in downplaying the incident and absolving the Christian Brothers, who had invested their own resources 'in a Christian endeavour to ameliorate certain conditions', from any blame. Moylan was unable to

> conceive any deliberate ill-treatment of boys by a community motivated by the ideals of its founder. I cannot conceive any sadism emanating from men who were trained to a life of sacrifice and of austerity. They are also trained to have great devotion to a very high purpose. The point is that accidents will happen in the best regulated families and in this family there are about 800 boys. Many of them were sent to Artane because of the difficulties of their character and because of a good deal of unruliness of conduct ... Because of the unfortunate background of many of these boys, possibly due to evil social conditions, Deputies must realise how careful the handling of them as a group must be and how far from easy it is to ensure the working of such an institution ... This is an isolated incident; it can only happen again as an accident ... I would point out to parents that any guarantee I give them of full protection for their children is no licence to any of the children to do what they like.[50]

Moylan's response was followed by the dissolution of the Dáil and the Artane incident was not revisited. The incident was examined by the Commission to Inquire into Child Abuse (CICA), known as the Ryan Commission, established by the government to investigate all forms of child abuse in Irish institutions from 1936 onwards. The commission's public report, commonly referred to as the Ryan report, was issued on 20 May 2009 and confirmed the details of what Cowan had revealed in the Dáil. At the first public hearing on 15 September 2005, Brother Reynolds, speaking on behalf of Christian Brothers, accepted that the incident was one of the most serious incidents involving the order and that 'it was handled badly, from all aspects of it'. The investigating committee concluded that the incident revealed a system that was deeply flawed, in which young, inexperienced brothers were left to cope with difficult children without adequate training, and without the support and supervision of a good management system. The failure to disclose the incident suggested that there was a policy of concealing damaging information.[51]

1954 GENERAL ELECTION

In the general election held on the 18 May 1954, Cowan attracted 2,353 first preference votes, 4.96 per cent of the total valid poll and just under 30 per cent of the quota. On this occasion Cowan was less transfer friendly and was eliminated after the tenth count. His final tally of 3,405 votes was over 4,300 short of gaining the fifth seat in the five-seat Dublin North-East constituency.[52] The loss of the seat ended Peadar Cowan's career as a parliamentarian. Between February 1948 and April 1954 his contributions to debates filled 29 columns in the Dáil debates index compared to 20 columns for John A. Costello. In addition, he made considerable contributions to the committee stage of the Irish News Agency Bill (1949), Transport Bill (1949) and Defence Bill (1951).[53] His range of contributions formed an eclectic mix and ranged from pressing the Taoiseach for a decision on the removal of a statue of Queen Victoria, 'a foreign monarch, from the Quadrangle at Leinster House', to emphasizing the necessity to set primary certificate examination in Ulster Irish for children from Ulster counties.[54] Over a few months in 1950, for example, he strongly supported the bill to provide a statutory six-day holiday with pay to the agricultural labourer ('he is treated like a slave'), questioned the need for American forces to pay 'courtesy visits to the country in atomic bomb carrying planes'; sought protection for tenants of local authority houses from eviction; and his contribution to the debate on the Nurses Bill (1949) at its second stage was measured and insightful. The bill was 'a step in the right direction'. 'It was vital that nursing conditions both in training and after training should be improved' if the flow of young girls to England to train as nurses was to be curbed. During training and later, nurses 'have been held almost as prisoners, subject to disciplinary regulations that were entirely out of date'. More theoretical training was essential. There was an urgent need to ensure that those who 'enter the nursing profession here are not treated as prisoners or as slaves. We must see that they get reasonable time to study, that there must be reasonable periods for lectures and theoretical training and reasonable hours of work'.[55] He also supported the Adoption Society (Ireland)'s unsuccessful quest for the introduction of legislation to legalize adoption in Ireland by asking parliamentary questions and informally lobbying the Minister for Justice, Seán MacEoin, on the issue. The minister eventually decided not to introduce any legislation that 'would provide for the irrevocable transfer of a parent's rights and duties in respect of a child to any other person'.[56]

A powerful contribution made in December 1948 was particularly notable when he challenged the failure of the inter-party government to deal with the 'bread and butter' issues and especially the problems of unemployment ('it is almost impossible to find employment for a person who is unemployed and who is anxious to get work of any kind'), housing shortage ('large families living in single rooms and in insanitary basements'), emigration, ministerial incompetence and army pensions. He questioned the role of the banks in making credit available only on 'impossible conditions'. Consequently private employers were unable to obtain capital and to build small establishments or small industries to provide employment. The old idea of free enterprise favoured by the government was no longer fit for purpose and he agreed with the ideas of Seán Lemass that industrial development needed government stimulus and government help. This contribution ended with a warning to small parties engaged in coalition governments that has stood the test of time: 'In a general way, the small Parties combined together in this inter-party government will sink together with the government. They will sink because of the failure of the government to do the job properly and because of the failure of the individual ministers to shoulder their responsibilities'.[57]

Conclusion

Peadar Cowan's final years in public life were difficult. The death of his wife, Rosemary, in October 1955 following a short illness was a devastating blow. According to his grandson, Rory, his world fell apart and he was unable to cope after Rosemary's death.[1] He resigned his seat on the Dublin Corporation in 1955 and was declared bankrupt in 1956. Worse was to follow. On 30 October 1957 he was convicted in the Dublin Central Criminal Court of the fraudulent conversion for his own use and benefit of a sum of £3,705, the property of one of his clients, James O'Reilly, a Dublin bricklayer. On 1 November 1957, he was sentenced to two years' imprisonment with hard labour and was refused leave to appeal.[2] This decision was unsuccessfully appealed to the Court of Criminal Appeal but the presiding judges referred the matter to the Supreme Court in their judgment issued on 20 December 1957, as the decision involved 'a point of exceptional public importance and that it was desirable in the public interest that an appeal there from should be taken to the Supreme Court.' This too was unsuccessful: all four judges found against Cowan in their judgment issued on 4 February 1958 and he was committed to prison. He was released from prison by order of the Minister for Justice on 16 January 1959.[3]

He was removed from the roll of solicitors by the chief justice on 31 October 1958. As a lawyer, Peadar Cowan built up a substantial portfolio of cases, defending those on the margins of society charged with criminal offences. He was also active in challenging eviction orders of the type outlined in the opening paragraph of this book. Given his military background he was also somewhat of a specialist in defending those charged with breaches of army discipline. In 1945, it was part of government policy to arrest former members of the Irish army who absented themselves without leave and joined the British army during the Second World War and charge them with desertion in courts martial. His defence of Patrick Shannon and Patrick Keogh in June 1945 was particularly noteworthy. Keogh, charged with desertion from July 1943, joined the Royal Air Force (RAF) and was engaged in several missions over Germany before he was shot down and became a prisoner of war. On his return to Ireland after his liberation by American forces, he was arrested and charged with desertion. Cross-examined by Cowan he explained that he joined the RAF 'to get a crack at Germany' because of the suffering of his relatives in England and because he opposed Nazism. In his defence, Cowan argued that he had left 'a post of safety for one of considerable danger', the reverse of what constitutes desertion. Any man who endangered his life to destroy what the Pope had described 'as the satanic spectre of Nazism should not receive punishment in any civilized country'. Cowan requested that Keogh be granted an immediate discharge from the army: 'In many countries and by a great many people in this country, the accused is not considered or could not be considered as a criminal meriting punishment but as a hero who deserves honours and rewards'. Patrick Shannon was charged with desertion from July 1941 when he joined the British Army and he too had spent time as prisoner of war. He was arrested on the Belfast–Dublin train as he returned on special compassionate leave to visit his seriously ill mother. Economic necessity forced Shannon to absent himself without leave, Cowan argued. He was unable to support his mother on his army pay of 14s. a week and joined the British army to remedy this situation. She then received an allowance of 14s. a week and out of his own daily pay of 7s. 9d. he was able to send her £5 every two weeks. In his submission, Cowan noted that, in the circumstances, 'the bringing of this charge was something they all ought to be utterly ashamed of'.[4] Both defendants were sentenced to 156 days detention, which was commuted in each case to discharge from the army.[5] It was a partial victory for Cowan; in August the government issued an Emergency Powers Order dismissing soldiers who were absent without leave for at least 180 days with forfeit of all pension rights as well as disqualifying them from holding any future employment in any state, local authority or statutory body or board.[6] Peadar Cowan scored a significant victory in another Emergency related trial in 1946 when one of his clients was cleared by the Court of Criminal Appeal on a charge of conspiracy and of selling sugar at a price in excess of the controlled price. Richard Kennedy was convicted and sentenced to 12 months imprisonment by the Special Criminal Court. It was a double victory as the state appeal to the Supreme Court also failed. In a preliminary issue, the court ruled that the Attorney-General did not have a right of appeal to that court 'on his own certificate' from a decision of the Court of Criminal Appeal quashing a conviction of the Special Criminal Appeal.[7]

Despite his financial and legal difficulties, Peadar Cowan was re-elected to the Dublin Corporation on the thirteenth and final count for Electoral Area No. 1 in 1960.[8] On the 13 July 1960, the validity of his election was challenged by a number of individuals on the basis that at the time of his election he was an undischarged bankrupt and ineligible to hold public office.[9] The three High Court judges on the rota for the trial of parliamentary election petitions nominated Richard N. Cooke, a practising barrister, to examine the petition. Cowan challenged the constitutionality of the 1882 Municipal Corporation (Ireland) Act and the Municipal Corporations (Corrupt and Illegal Practices) Act 1884 relating to the appointment of barristers as commissioners for the trial of election petitions. This time he was successful and won an important legal victory as Justice Haugh found that the proposed petition was repugnant to and *ultra vires* the Constitution on the basis that the election court 'might make findings which would affect the life, liberties, fortunes or reputations of individuals; and the election court might exercise its jurisdiction in matters partly criminal'. Consequently sections of the Local Government Acts of 1941 and 1946 were declared unconstitutional. Cowan was also granted an injunction that prevented the continuance of the petition and consequently he retained his Dublin Corporation seat.[10]

Peadar Cowan planned to contest the general election of 1961 as an independent candidate and this required another visit to the courts. As an undischarged bankrupt, he petitioned the High Court for a certificate of conformity but was refused by Justice Kenny. Evidence was presented that the final stage of the bankruptcy proceedings had been completed and that a dividend of 6s. 8d. in the £1 had been paid to Cowan's creditors on the proven debts of £8,000 and that a further payment of up to 4s. was possible out of the funds in court. A twenty-one day notice to creditors was essential to achieve a discharge but in Cowan's case this was not possible because of the election date. An appeal of Justice Kenny's decision to a special sitting of the Supreme Court also failed.[11] Regardless of the legal setbacks, Cowan contested the 1961 general election as an independent candidate in the Dublin North-East constituency but his first preference poll of 1,863, just 4.4 per cent of the valid poll, was well short of the minimum necessary for election.[12]

DUNGEONS DEEP

Peadar Cowan drew on his personal experiences of the Irish prison system for his final significant contribution to public life. In 1960, he published *Dungeons deep*, a 48-page booklet in which he combined his personal experience, his knowledge of the legal system and his legal expertise to produce a remarkable exposé of the Irish prison and reformatory system, 'a system that confirmed the view of many enlightened foreigners that Ireland is one of the last remaining bastions of reaction in a progressive and progressing world'. Laced with political invective aimed at the minister and the Department of Justice and statistical detail, as well as social awareness and concern, it was an extraordinary and enlightened publication that included several suggestions for reform of the penal system in Ireland.

Conditions in Mountjoy were the main focus of Cowan's attention. Tribute was paid to the governor and to the humanity and general decency of the officers who worked under severe constraints. The absence of segregation in the prison and the inclusion of remand prisoners with the general prison population outraged him: 'the raper, the sodomist, the sexual offender, the defiler of little children, the bestial brute, and the incestuous beast are placed in association with men who have had the misfortune to be imprisoned for a motoring or customs or other offence of this type and with youths in their early twenties and others imprisoned for minor offences'. This system existed because the 'Ministry of Justice had an antediluvian notion of its moral responsibilities'. Prison clothing is 'often stained, torn, dirty, ill-fitting and trampish looking'. The food supplied to the prisoners was 'poor, inadequate, monotonous, and incapable of maintaining human beings in health'. The dietary regime prescribed by the minister was 'contrary to the moral law': 'No Dublin housewife would cook some of the mutton that went into a prison stew even if she got it for nothing'. Meals were served on plates that sometimes 'leaked as a result of rust eating through the metal where the enamel had chipped or broken off'.[13]

Cowan provided an in-depth profile of the physical infrastructure of Mountjoy prison; the prison hospital, 'starved of funds for modernization, [was] a frowsy dump'. Appropriate segregation was non-existent and 'To be placed in the position of having to walk around the prison hospital recreation yard with a person who had, in a fit of madness, killed a dear one, or with another, who had in an insane frenzy, made a murderous assault on a friend or neighbour is an experience that ought not to be forced on a sensitive prisoner'. Hospital patients were allowed a bath once a fortnight; those in the main prison are allowed a weekly bath. 'No bath towel [was] issued to the patients who have to dry themselves with their soiled sheets'. Consequently the baths were given on sheet changing day. According to Cowan's account a patient was frequently employed as the hospital cook and left in sole charge of the kitchen. Dental treatment was limited to extraction; the prisoner was required to pay for all other treatment. 'It [was] really difficult to imagine how out of touch with modern ideas the Department of Justice [was] and how little it appeared to know of the work, activities, policy and efforts of other government departments and governments in the field of health, and social welfare. As far as the Department of Justice is concerned this might still be the Stone Age'. The bakery of four turf or wooden ovens was antiquated. Only two of the ovens were in working order and these were 'nearing the end of their tether'.[14]

Unfortunately, like the Artane incident described in the previous chapter, Peadar Cowan's views on industrial schools and reformatories were confirmed decades later when stories of the abuse of young residents in some of these institutions emerged and were confirmed. In the 1990s, documentary makers and victims of abuse in various institutions managed by religious orders unravelled a series of brutal hidden Irelands stretching back many decades and in May 1999, the government apologized to the victims.[15] In *Dungeons deep* Cowan's verdict was damning: 'industrial schools and reformatories can be a positive danger to the children sent to them'. The system of bullying that existed and was officially approved 'made bullies, gangsters, liars, deceivers, and enemies of society out of many of the other boys'. A culture of secrecy existed; 'allegations of homosexuality were widespread'. 'There is a tendency to hide from the public, knowledge of any incident of unnatural practice in

CONDITIONS IN MOUNTJOY PRISON

Peadar Cowan, 182 Killester Ave., Dublin, writes in the course of a letter: I had to wait until to-day (Wednesday) for the official report of the Dáil debate on my small book, "Dungeons Deep.' The Minister for Justice is quoted at col. 656-7 as saying: " I do not believe for a moment, from my own personal experience, having visited the prison on a number of occasions, that there is an atom of truth in the statements in the book." I now challenge the Minister to establish a judicial tribunal to enquire into the matter when I will prove not only the truth of my statements but the fact that the Minister conveyed a fandango of misleading information to the Dáil.

As to the Minister's personal experience of conditions in Mountjoy Prison nowadays, I will say that to my own knowledge he made one cursory inspection during the first two years of his office as Minister for Justice. Perhaps he will tell us how many inspections he made of the prison during the last fifteen months

5. Peadar Cowan's response to Oscar Traynor's Dáil comments on *Dungeons deep*
(*Irish Independent*, 7 July 1960)

institutions to which children are committed by the courts'. In Cowan's view, few boys benefited from their retention in a reformatory and during his career as a lawyer he was proactive in rescuing children from such a fate. If the system of industrial schools was to be retained as 'a temporary or transient expedient' it was better 'if the Catholic boys were placed in under the care and guardianship of Nuns instead of Brothers as at present nuns could be relied on to treat the children with kindness, and to give them the love and appreciation they need'. He noted that 'the Brothers in charge, all holy men, are looked upon as jailers by the children who come to associate in their minds religion with repression'.[16]

This searing, early 1960s example of speaking truth to power was rejected by those in authority. The work was dismissed. 'I do not believe ... that there is an atom of truth in the statements in the book. I believe it is done purely for the sake of personal publicity' was the response of Oscar Traynor, the Minister for Justice. Cowan challenged Traynor to establish a judicial tribunal he claimed would establish 'the truth of my statements but also the fact that the minister conveyed a fandango of misleading information to the Dáil' (fig. 5).[17]

Not all deputies agreed with Traynor's dismissal of the book and its contents. Fine Gael TD, James Dillon, in particular, read extensive sections of the book into the Dáil record during the debate on the Criminal Justice Bill (1960) and drew the attention of the deputies to the conditions described by Cowan. William Norton urged Traynor 'not to write off the pamphlet as of no consequence'. Cowan's 'claims ought to be checked and they ought to be answered'.[18]

'PERSONALLY AN ABLE FELLOW'

This was Cowan's last significant contribution to the political discourse of the day. He died on 7 May 1962 after a short illness leaving an estate valued at £5.[19] According to the *Irish Independent* 'he was one of Dublin's best known public figures'; Maurice Dockrell, a Fine Gael TD, was generous in his tribute and regretted the passing of a 'fearless champion of many causes'.[20] A report compiled in the 1940s was prophetic as Cowan demonstrated in his parliamentary career.

A man with 'plenty of initiative and drive' according to police reports, 'he may be classified as a man of immense political ambition and having regard to the fact that he is personally an able fellow, he is a man to be reckoned with. However he is rather pugnacious and truculent in manner and this may prove a set-back in his political career'.[21]

Cowan's restless spirit was inspired by a keenly informed social conscience and much of his maverick political meandering was driven by a regard for social justice and the courage to fearlessly pursue his convictions regardless of the personal cost. Peadar Cowan's radical thought challenged the consensus and frequently led to his political isolation. His concern for the poor and marginalized of society was the great consistency of his political career. He joined the Labour Party because 'he could not stand aside and see the hunger, squalor and misery in this country, while the two big parties were cutting one another's throats'. It is ironic that Peadar Cowan died in poverty in 1962. His championing of socialism was not a popular cause in the 1940s or 1950s and as we have seen he was frequently on the defensive against charges that he was a communist and interested in promoting communism. His nationalist thought evolved over the thirty years or so of his political career. His journey from accepting the Anglo-Irish Treaty of 1921 and its limited form of independence to the belief that political unity could only be achieved by physical force led him down the road of political ridicule when he attempted to assemble a force in 1950 to invade and reclaim Northern Ireland. This journey began with a decade's immersion in cultural nationalism through the medium of the GAA as he encouraged the development of a self-contained Ireland with its own culture and its own distinctive civilisation. Finally, Cowan became part of the radical left tradition of the Irish nationalist conglomerate. Political unity on its own was of little value unless it was accompanied by a social revolution that eliminated poverty and inequality to be achieved by socialist revolution.

In the final analysis, Peadar Cowan was the ultimate outsider: an army officer from a working class background with a social conscience; the native of Co. Cavan who transformed the GAA in Co. Westmeath while a non-resident in the county for most of the time he was active as an administrator; a radical socialist in the Labour Party without any union background; a former Irish Free State officer surrounded by IRA veterans in Clann na Poblachta; a challenger of the consensus in Dáil Éireann and an ex-army officer, solicitor and parliamentarian who was declared bankrupt, served a prison sentence and used the experience to write a seminal exposé of prison conditions and advocate for prison reform. Peadar Cowan's final years, lived in poverty, were unfortunate for a man of considerable moral courage who made a substantial contribution to public debate during his career.

Notes

ABBREVIATIONS

AAA   Army Athletic Association
CBMB   County Board Minute Book
CPI   Communist Party of Ireland
DIB   James McGuire and James Quinn (eds), *Dictionary of Irish biography: from the earliest times to the year 2002* (Cambridge, 2009), 9 vols
GAA   Gaelic Athletic Association
IMA   Irish Medical Association
INTO   Irish National Teachers' Organisation
IRA   Irish Republican Army
ITGWU   Irish Transport and General Workers' Union
RAF   Royal Air Force
RPRA   Republican Prisoners' Release Association
TD   Teachta Dála
UCDSHA   UCD Archives, School of History and Archives

INTRODUCTION

1   Eamon Dunphy, *The rocky road* (Dublin, 2014), pp 32–4.
2   *Irish Press*, 30 Nov. 1936.
3   *Longford Leader*, 12 May 1962.
4   Eithne MacDermott, *Clann na Poblachta* (Cork, 1998), pp 17, 81, 137.
5   Kevin Rafter, *The Clann: the story of Clann na Poblachta* (Dublin, 1996), p. 40.
6   David McCullagh, *A makeshift majority: the first inter-party government, 1948–51* (Dublin, 1998).
7   J.H. Whyte, *Church & state in modern Ireland, 1923–1979* (Dublin, 1980), pp 240-6, 264–7.
8   Paul Daly, Ronan O'Brien and Paul Rouse (eds), *Making the difference: the Irish Labour Party, 1912–2012* (Cork, 2012).
9   MacDermott, *Clann na Poblachta*, p. 39.

I. ARMY OFFICER AND GAA ADMINISTRATOR

1   Military Archives (MA), Abstract of service for Captain Peter Cowan.
2   Pauric J. Dempsey, 'Cowan, Peadar' *Dictionary of Irish biography (DIB)*, 2 (2009), pp 925–6; *An t-Óglác*, 15 Dec.

1923; www.MilitaryArchives.ie/Irish Army Census Records, p. 48.
3   *Labour News*, 12 Mar. 1938.
4   *Irish Times*, 26 Oct. 1938.
5   *An t-Óglác*, 5 July 1924.
6   Ibid., 7 Apr. 1923.
7   *Irish Independent*, 13, 23 Feb., 26 Apr. 1943.
8   *Westmeath Independent*, 24 Apr. 1926.
9   *Westmeath Examiner*, 22 Feb. 1930.
10 County Board Minute Book (CBMB), 31 Jan. 1932.
11 *Westmeath Examiner*, 1 Feb. 1930.
12 Ibid., 19 Sept. 1936.
13 CBMB, minute of 29 Jan. 1928.
14 *Westmeath Examiner*, 1 Feb. 1930.
15 CBMB, 26 Feb. 1928, 20 Feb. 1929.
16 *Midland Reporter*, 19 Oct. 1933.
17 CBMB, 8 Dec. 1933.
18 *Westmeath Examiner*, 15 Sept. 1934, 22 Sept. 1938; *Westmeath Independent*, 29 Sept. 1928, 17 Nov. 1928, 2 Feb. 1929.
19 CBMB, minute of 29 Jan.1933.
20 CBMB, minute of 3 Jan. 1933.
21 Ibid.
22 *Irish Press*, 13 Dec. 1934.
23 *Westmeath Independent*, 2 Feb. 1929.

24 Ibid., 24 Mar. 1928.
25 *Westmeath Examiner*, 1 Feb. 1930.
26 Ibid., 12 Apr. 1930.
27 Ibid., 26 Apr. 1930.
28 *Westmeath Independent*, 16 Feb. 1935, 27 Apr. 1935.
29 *Westmeath Examiner*, 26 Apr. 1930.
30 Ibid., 6 Feb. 1932.
31 *Midland Reporter*, 4 Feb. 1932.
32 Ibid.
33 Ibid.
34 *Midland Reporter*, 18 Sept. 1930, 9 Apr. 1931, 16 Apr. 1931, 21 May 1931, 4 June 1931, 18 June 1931, 9 July 1931.
35 CBMB, minute of 14 Jan. 1934.
36 *Midland Reporter*, 10 Mar. 1932, 2 Feb. 1933.
37 *Midland Reporter*, 28 July 1932.
38 Ibid., 4 Oct. 1932.
39 Ibid., 15 Sept. 1932.
40 Ibid., 20 July 1933.
41 CBMB, minute of 14 Jan. 1934.
42 *Souvenir of official opening Cusack memorial park, Mullingar.*
43 Ibid.
44 CBMB, minute of 14 Jan. 1934.
45 *Irish Press*, 20 Mar. 1933.
46 *Midland Reporter*, 29 June 1933.
47 R.V. Comerford, *Ireland: inventing the nation* (London, 2003), p. 116.
48 *Westmeath Examiner*, 22 July 1933.
49 CBMB, minute of 14 Jan. 1934.
50 Ibid.
51 *Westmeath Examiner*, 12 Aug. 1933.
52 *Midland Reporter*, 10 Aug. 1933.
53 CBMB, 2 Sept. 1933.
54 CBMB, 4 Aug. 1933.
55 *Irish Press*, 28 Oct. 1936.
56 See Tom Hunt, 'Cusack Park Mullingar: the conception, difficult gestation and spectacular delivery of a GAA venue', *Ríocht na Midhe*, 18 (2006), pp 271–91, for a detailed account of the development of Cusack Park.

2. PEADAR COWAN AND THE LABOUR PARTY

1 UCD Archives, School of History and Archives (UCDSHA), Sean MacEntee Papers, P67/545.
2 MacDermott, *Clann na Poblachta*, p. 7.
3 Charlie McGuire, *Roddy Connolly and the struggle for socialism in Ireland* (Cork, 2008), pp 142–55.
4 *Offaly Independent*, 26 June 1937.

5 *Labour News*, 22 May, 11 Sept. 1937.
6 Ferghal McGarry, 'Catholics first and politicians afterwards': the Labour Party and the workers' republic, 1936–39, *Saothar*, 25 (2000), p. 57.
7 *Drogheda Independent*, 5 June, 26 June 1937.
8 McCullagh, *De Valera, Volume II: Rule, 1932–75* (Dublin, 2018), p. 55.
9 *Offaly Independent*, 26 June 1937. Mr Kennedy was a Fianna Fáil TD for the constituency.
10 *Meath Chronicle*, 26 June 1937.
11 Niamh Puirséil, 'Religion and the Labour Party' in Paul Daly, Ronán O'Brien & Paul Rouse (eds), *Making the difference? the Irish Labour Party, 1919–2012* (Dublin, 2012), p. 183.
12 *Meath Chronicle*, 10 July 1937.
13 *Labour News*, 16 Oct. 1937.
14 Ibid., 16 Oct. 1937, 22 Jan. 1938.
15 Ibid., 20 Nov. 1937.
16 John A. Murphy, *Ireland in the twentieth century* (Dublin, 1975), p. 94.
17 McCullagh, *De Valera II*, p. 150.
18 *The Liberator*, 28 May 1938.
19 *Westmeath Examiner*, 4 June 1938.
20 *Meath Chronicle*, 18 June 1938.
21 *Westmeath Examiner*, 11 June 1938.
22 *Meath Chronicle*, 25 June 1938.
23 *Irish Times*, 21 Aug. 1942; Diarmaid Ferriter, *The transformation of Ireland* (Wisconsin, 2007), p. 413; *Westmeath Examiner*, 14 Feb. 1942.
24 *Drogheda Independent*, 13 Mar. 1943; *Irish Press*, 11 Mar. 1943
25 *Meath Chronicle*, 30 Jan. 1943.
26 Ibid., 30 Jan. 1943, 27 Feb. 1943.
27 Ibid., 12 June 1943.
28 *Westmeath Independent*, 12 June 1943.
29 Ibid., 19 June 1943.
30 *Connaught Telegraph*, 6 Feb. 1943; *Donegal Democrat*, 12 June 1943; *Sligo Champion*, 19 June 1943.
31 *Meath Chronicle*, 3 July 1943.
32 McCullagh, *De Valera II*, pp 236–7.
33 Fearghal McGarry, 'Catholics first and politicians afterwards', pp 63–4.
34 Niamh Puirséil, '"If it's socialism you want, join some other party": Labour and the left' in Daly, O'Brien & Rouse (eds), *Making the difference?*, p. 72.
35 *Irish Press*, 17 Feb. 1943.
36 Puirséil, 'If it's socialism you want', pp 72–3

37 *Tuam Herald*, 26 Feb. 1944.
38 Ibid., 2 Mar. 1944.
39 Emmet O'Connor, 'Anti-communism in twentieth-century Ireland', *Twentieth Century Communism*, 6 (2014), pp 69–71.
40 *Meath Chronicle*, 9 July 1938.
41 *Drogheda Independent*, 2 July 1938.
42 *Meath Chronicle*, 30 Jan. 1943.
43 McCullagh, *De Valera II*, p. 245.
44 *Irish Times*, 27 May 1944.
45 *Irish Independent*, 22 May 1944.
46 *Meath Chronicle*, 27 May, 3 June 1944; *Drogheda Independent*, 27 May 1944.
47 Ibid., 3 June 1944.
48 McCullagh, *De Valera II*, p. 247.
49 *Irish Press*, 21 Aug. 1944; *Tuam Herald*, 21 Oct. 1944.
50 *Irish Press*, 23 Sept. 1944.
51 *Irish Times*, 13 Oct. 1944.
52 Ibid., 28 Oct. 1944.
53 Ibid., 5 Oct. 1944.
54 *Irish Press*, 14 Oct. 1944; *Irish Times*, 13 Oct. 1944.
55 *Irish Press*, 9 Mar. 1946; UCDSHA, MacEntee Papers, P67/548.
56 *Irish Times*, 29 Apr. 1946.
57 UCDSHA. MacEntee Papers, P67/551.

3. PEADAR COWAN AND CLANN NA POBLACHTA

1 McCullagh, *De Valera II*, p. 178.
2 *Irish Times*, 22 June 1945.
3 Rafter, *The Clann*, p. 18.
4 J. Bowyer Bell, *The secret army, the IRA, 1916–1979* (Cambridge, MA, 1983), pp 242–3.
5 *Evening Herald*, 4 May 1946; *Irish Examiner*, 27 May 1946; *Munster Express*, 7 June 1946; *Nenagh Guardian*, 8 June 1946; *Connacht Sentinel*, 25 June 1946; *Connacht Tribune*, 29 June 1946.
6 *Drogheda Independent*, 25 May 1946.
7 *Irish Times*, 22 June 1945.
8 Barry Flynn, *Pawns in the game: Irish hunger strikes, 1912–1981* (Cork, 2011), pp 107–10.
9 *Drogheda Independent*, 25 May 1946.
10 *Waterford News*, 31 May 1946.
11 *The Nationalist*, 8 June 1946.
12 *Irish Press*, 7 June 1946.
13 Ibid., 7 June 1946.
14 Caitriona Lawlor (ed.), *Seán MacBride: that day's struggle, a memoir, 1994–1951* (Dublin, 2005), p. 130.
15 Lawlor, *MacBride*, p. 130.

16 *Irish Press*, 29 June 1943.
17 *Irish Times*, 8 July 1946.
18 Rafter, *Clann*, p. 23.
19 MacDermott, *Clann na Poblachta*, pp 15–16.
20 Lawlor, *MacBride*, pp 214–15.
21 *Irish Independent*, 14 Apr. 1947
22 *Nenagh Guardian*, 17 May 1947; *Irish Times*, 22 May 1947.
23 *Irish Times*, 2 June 1947.
24 Ibid.
25 Ibid., 25 June 1947.
26 *Irish Independent*, 28 July 1947.
27 McCullagh, *De Valera II*, p. 247.
28 *Irish Press*, 14 July 1947.
29 Rafter, *Clann*, p. 52.
30 McCullagh, *De Valera II*, p. 286.
31 *Irish Press*, 1 Dec. 1947.
32 *Cork Examiner*, 1 Dec. 1947.
33 Rafter, *Clann*, pp 52-4.
34 McCullagh, *De Valera II*, p. 286.
35 Ibid., p. 287.
36 *Irish Press*, 15 Dec. 1947.
37 Ibid., 22 Dec. 1947.
38 Ibid., 16, 18 Dec. 1947.
39 *Irish Times*, 12, 16 Jan. 1948.
40 *Irish Press*, 20 Jan. 1948.
41 *Irish Times*, 31 Jan. 1948.
42 UCDSHA, MacEntee Papers, P67/548.
43 Rafter, *Clann*, p. 77.
44 UCDSHA, MacEntee Papers, P67/548
45 Ibid., P67/551.
46 Ibid.
47 *Irish Press*, 13 Dec. 1947.
48 McCullagh, *De Valera II*, p. 287.
49 *Irish Press*, 17 Jan. 1948.
50 Ibid., 20, 21 Jan. 1948.
51 Ibid., 29 Jan. 1948.
52 McCullagh, *De Valera II*, pp 290–1.
53 Vincent Browne (ed.), *The Magill book of Irish politics* (Dublin, 1981), p. 124.
54 Donnacha Ó Beacháin, *Destiny of the soldiers, Fianna Fáil, Irish republicanism and the IRA, 1926–1973* (Dublin, 2010), p. 215; MacEntee Papers, P67/547.
55 Dermot Keogh, *Twentieth-century Ireland, nation and state* (Dublin, 1994), p. 5.
56 *Irish Times*, 13 July 1948.
57 *Irish Press*, 5 July 1948.
58 MacDermott, *Clann na Poblachta*, p. 80.
59 *Cork Examiner*, 5 July 1948.
60 Ibid., 5 July 1948; David McCullagh, *A makeshift majority* (Dublin, 1998), pp 233–4.

61 J.J. Lee, *Ireland, 1912–1985* (Dublin, 1989), p. 304.
62 *Dáil Debates*, 1 July 1948.
63 *Cork Examiner*, 5 July 1948.
64 *Irish Times*, 12 July 1948.
65 *Cork Examiner*, 5 July 1948; *Irish Press*, 5 July 1948.

4. THE INDEPENDENT DÁIL DEPUTY

1 McCullagh, *Makeshift majority*, pp 82–5.
2 *Dáil Debates*, vol. 112, no. 9, 28 July 1948.
3 Ibid., 5 Aug. 1948.
4 McCullagh, *Makeshift majority*, p. 126.
5 *Irish Press*, 6 June 1949.
6 Ronan Fanning, *Éamon de Valera: a will to power* (Dublin, 2013), p. 229.
7 *Irish Times*, 6 Feb. 1950.
8 Ibid., 16 May 1950.
9 Ibid., 10 July 1950.
10 Ibid., 20 May 1950.
11 Ibid., 20 June 1950.
12 Ibid., 27 June 1950.
13 *Dáil Debates*, vol. 122, no. 6, 7 July 1950.
14 Ibid., vol. 122, no. 7, 11 July 1950.
15 *Irish Times*, 15, 29 Nov. 1950.
16 Lee, *Ireland 1912–1985*, p. 313.
17 Ibid., p. 316; John A. Murphy, *Ireland in the twentieth century* (Dublin, 1975), p. 131; McCullagh, *Makeshift majority*, pp 215–16.
18 *Irish Times*, 7 Mar. 1951.
19 Whyte, *Church and state*, pp 224–8.
20 Ibid., p. 241.
21 Ibid., see pp 419–48 for the complete correspondence relating to the matter.
22 Tom Garvin, *News from a new republic: Ireland in the 1950s* (Dublin, 2011), p. 38.
23 *Irish Times*, 12 Apr. 1951.
24 *Dáil Debates*, vol. 125, no. 5, 12 Apr. 1951.
25 MacDermott, *Clann na Poblachta*, p. 80; *Irish Times*, 4 Feb. 1950.
26 John Horgan, *Noël Browne, passionate outsider* (Dublin, 2000), p. 158.
27 *Dáil Debates*, vol. 125, no. 5, 12 Apr. 1951.
28 Ibid.
29 Ibid., vol. 125, no. 6, 17 Apr. 1951.
30 Noël Browne, *Against the tide* (Dublin, 1986), p. 7.
31 *Dáil Debates*, vol. 125, no. 6, 17 Apr. 1951.
32 Ibid.
33 Ibid.
34 McCullagh, *Makeshift majority*, p. 248.

35 *Irish Press*, 1, 2 June 1951.
36 *Longford Leader*, 23 Sep. 1951.
37 *Irish Times*, 2 June 1951.
38 *Irish Press*, 14 June 1951.
39 *Dáil Debates*, vol. 126, no. 1, 13 June 1951.
40 Ibid.
41 Ibid.
42 *Dáil Debates*, vol. 135, no. 8, 4 Dec. 1952.
43 Ibid., vol. 138, no. 4, 22 Apr. 1953.
44 Michael Kennedy and Eunan O'Halpin, *Ireland and the Council of Europe: from isolation towards integration* (Strasbourg, 2000), pp 97–9.
45 *Sunday Independent*, 27 Sept. 1953.
46 Ibid., 4 Oct. 1953.
47 Kennedy and O'Halpin, *Ireland and the Council of Europe*, p. 99.
48 *Dáil Debates*, vol. 145, no. 7, 23 Apr. 1954.
49 Aideen Carroll, *Seán Moylan, rebel leader*, (Cork, 2010), p. 255.
50 *Dáil Debates*, vol. 145, no. 7, 23 Apr. 1954.
51 Ryan Commission, *Report of commission to inquire into child abuse*, vol. 1, chapter 7, 112–37.
52 *Irish Press*, 20 May 1954.
53 Dempsey, 'Cowan, Peadar', *DIB*, pp 925–6.
54 Rafter, *Clann*, p. 130.
55 *Dáil Debates*, vol. 119, no. 8, 2 Mar. 1950; vol. 123, no. 8, 23 Nov. 1950; vol. 122, no. 8, 6 July 1950; vol. 123, no. 3, 8 Nov. 1950.
56 Whyte, *Church and state*, pp 185–7. *Dáil Debates*, vol. 123, no. 9, 29 Nov. 1950.
57 *Dáil Debates*, vol. 113, no. 3, 16 Dec. 1948.

5. CONCLUSION

1 *Anglo-Celt*, 19 Nov. 1955; *Rory Cowan: Mrs Cowan's boy* (Dublin, 2019), pp 18–21.
2 *Irish Independent*, 31 Oct., 2 Nov. 1957.
3 *Irish Law Times Report*, The People v Peadar Cowan, 4 Feb. 1958. Dempsey, 'Cowan', *DIB*, p. 926.
4 *Evening Echo*, 12 June 1945.
5 *Belfast Newsletter*, 18 June 1945.
6 *Irish Times*, 9 Aug. 1945.
7 *Irish Press*, 1 Feb. 1946.
8 *Irish Press*, 25 June 1960.
9 Ibid., 22 Sept. 1960.
10 *Irish Law Times Report*, pp 411–25.
11 *Cork Examiner*, 21, 23 Sept. 1961.

12 Ibid., 6 Oct. 1961.
13 Peadar Cowan, *Dungeons deep* (Dublin, 1960), pp 4–8.
14 Ibid., pp 12–17.
15 Ferriter, *The transformation of Ireland*, pp 736–7.
16 Cowan, *Dungeons deep*, pp 29–36.

17 *Irish Independent*, 7 July 1960.
18 *Dáil Debates*, vol. 183, no. 5, 28, 29 June 1960.
19 Dempsey, 'Cowan', *DIB*, p. 926.
20 *Irish Independent*, 8 May 1962.
21 UCDSHA, MacEntee Papers, P67/551.